Parenting Young Children with Love, Encouragement, and Limits

Thomas J. Dishion
Scot G. Patterson

Research Press · 2612 North Mattis Avenue, Champaign, Illinois 61822 · (800) 519-2707 · www.researchpress.com

5   4   3   2   1   05   06   07   08   09

Originally published by Castalia Publishing Company in 1996
under the title *Preventive Parenting with Love, Encouragement,
and Limits.*

Composition by Publication Services, Inc.
Cover design by Linda Brown, Positive I.D. Graphic Design, Inc.
Printed by United Graphics, Inc.

ISBN 0–87822–518–8
Library of Congress Control Number 2004113025

To Jacob and Briana, my greatest teachers
about parenthood

—Tom

To Miles and Kobin, for helping me become
a better father

—Scot

Contents

Preface

Parenting Young Children with Love, Encouragement, and Limits is a practical, future-oriented guide to raising toddlers and preschool-age children. The step-by-step approach presented in this book explains how to handle everyday problems, promote the well-being of your children, and create a positive family atmosphere. Our goal is to help you face the challenges of parenting with skill and confidence.

Parents are the key to helping children realize their potential for loving, learning, playing, and working. Infants and toddlers need to learn a wide range of skills from their parents to prepare them for their experiences outside the home. Recent studies have consistently shown a strong link between parenting practices and almost every aspect of children's development: their self-esteem, language development, achievement in school, success in forming friendships, and overall emotional adjustment. It is clear that parents play a crucial role in guiding their children's future.

Happy, well-adjusted children come from homes that provide a balanced mixture of *love, encouragement,* and *limits.* We have included these words in the title of this book to emphasize our commitment to the important skills they represent. There is no replacement for a parent's love—it is the wellspring of the lifetime of patience and caring that it takes to be a good parent. Encouragement provides support for the positive efforts of toddlers and young children, and it gives them the self-confidence they need to learn new skills during this period of rapid development. Parents also need to know how to set consistent limits to prevent or correct children's misbehavior. Effective limit setting includes the use of brief, mild consequences to back up household rules and to help children develop self-control. These three skills are the foundation for successful parenting.

Every parent knows that raising young children isn't easy. With this in mind, we have attempted to present the best information we could find on parenting skills that work. The methods described are based on the authors' experience as parents, insights from helping hundreds of troubled families in therapy sessions, and current research in child psychology. We have tried to present this information in friendly, nontechnical language to make the concepts easy for parents to understand and use.

How to Use This Book

We realize that parents of young children don't have much free time, so this book consists of short chapters that take only about 10 minutes to read. It's important to follow through on your reading by doing the home practice activities at the end of each chapter. The activities are divided into two sections: a basic skill and an advanced skill. Work on the basic skill first, then try the advanced skill if you have time. The exercises will help you get into the habit of using these new techniques in your daily family life. With practice, you will automatically choose the right course of action when a difficult situation arises.

This book can be used in several ways. Because developing parenting skills is hard work that requires support, some parents may use this book in parenting groups designed to provide guidance and encouragement. Others may want to work through this book individually with a therapist or counselor who has the necessary training in behavior therapy to help them apply the concepts presented here. Parents who use this book as a self-help guide should involve their partner or team up with a friend who has young children and work through the chapters in the order in which they are presented; the sequence of chapters has been carefully selected based on our work with hundreds of families over the years. Because preventive parenting involves using all of the skills described, it is better to read the entire book than to skip from chapter to chapter as a particular need arises.

We have tried to present a flexible approach to parenting that allows for a wide range of parenting styles and family situations. There is no single solution to the issues that arise in parenting or family living. Our goal is to give you the tools and information you need to do your best as a parent—the rest is up to you. If you have time now to read the first chapter, let's get started!

Acknowledgments

In many respects, this book is based on the work of our colleagues at the Oregon Social Learning Center, in Eugene. In particular, we are indebted to Dr. Gerald Patterson, whose work over the past four decades has pioneered a better understanding of both how families work and how they change. He is also acknowledged for his roles as mentor to Tom and mentor and father to Scot.

One of the unique aspects of the Oregon Social Learning Center is that it functions as a mission-oriented group. The contribution of any one of its members is heavily linked to the work of the group. Among those we would like to acknowledge as coauthors of sorts are Drs. Deborah Capaldi, Patricia Chamberlain, Bev Fagot, Marion Forgatch, Kate Kavanagh, and John Reid.

The list of others who have contributed to our understanding of families includes Drs. Russell Barkley, Diana Baumrind, Rex Forehand, Willard Hartup, Robert McMahon, Barbara Rogoff, and Carolyn Webster-Stratton.

INTRODUCTION

Exploring Your Role as a Parent

The scene. Mom and Dad look on as Ana cautiously moves away from the couch. She's standing on her own! Dad smiles as he holds out his arms and exclaims, "Come to papa!" Ana takes four teetering steps . . . and she's there. Dad and Mom look at each other and laugh—they can't believe that Ana has just taken her first steps. By the end of the afternoon, Ana is walking back and forth from Mom to Dad on the living room floor. During the course of this day, family life has turned another page.

Watching your child walk for the first time is a cherished moment. It also signals the beginning of a new stage of development, both for your child and for the rest of the family. Development means *change,* and it's up to the parents to guide the way in which these changes affect their family.

Your Child's First Six Years

These are the years of rapid and dramatic changes, not only for your child but for you as a parent. During the first few months your job is to feed and nurture your wonderful yet demanding baby. Gradually, you learn to tune in to your baby's crying, expressions, and patterns of sleeping and waking so that you can understand and attend to the baby's needs. During the first year of parenting, you develop "radar" that

1

tracks your baby at all times, *even when you're sleeping.* You're literally on call 24 hours a day.

When your baby begins to walk, it's a milestone for your child and for you as well. This is when the parenting practices described in this book become important. As your child grows and changes, you will need to adjust your approach to parenting to keep pace. That's what makes raising children interesting—things never stay the same for long.

As we mentioned earlier, the more effort you put into raising your children now, the easier your job will be in the future. You can never start too early. Studies have shown that the better we take care of a baby's needs during the first six months, the less the baby will cry and demand from us in the second year. This is very important. Your attention and care during the toddler and preschool years will make family life more enjoyable when your children are older. The same is true for each stage of childhood. Although the immediate rewards aren't obvious, your children will be happier and more secure if you get off to a good start and stay on track.

Preventive Parenting

This book addresses both the short-term and long-term effects of your approach to parenting. This approach requires that you pay attention to your children's needs, interests, and behaviors and carefully consider what they are learning from the way you respond to key events.

Although many aspects of raising children are just common sense, problems often arise when parents become too focused on short-term goals. This sets the stage for *accidental training,* which teaches children that they can get what they want by whining, crying, hitting, or having frequent temper tantrums. These problems are deceptive because they develop so slowly; it may take months or even years before parents realize that something is wrong. Gradually, however, the child's unpleasant behavior begins to take a toll on family life. As the child becomes increasingly out of control, his parents begin to receive reports from daycare and preschool staff that their child is disruptive or difficult to manage. Reading this book will help you *prevent* problems that would otherwise make everyone in the family miserable.

Believe it or not, preventive parenting begins with the simple interactions that you have with your infant or young child. These exchanges become routines that you repeat hundreds of times every day. For example, your baby smiles and you smile back, or your toddler says "bobo" and you respond with "Do you want your bottle?" Although these patterns may seem unimportant, they are your child's first lessons in using language and social skills. This modest beginning sets the stage for how well your child will get along with the children and adults he meets outside the home. Will your child be cooperative or difficult to live with? Will she make friends easily or be rejected by her peers? Will he do well in school or have trouble learning? These important features of your child's life are being shaped now, and you are in the driver's seat. This book will give you the information you need to make good choices for your child's future.

Common Obstacles to Effective Parenting

In therapy sessions with parents, we see that family life can become disrupted despite their good intentions. All parents want the best for their children. Why, then, is it so difficult for parents to keep everything in balance? Let's briefly review some of the issues that confront parents today.

There are many trends in our modern society that threaten the well-being of the family: the high rate of divorce, the dramatic increase in the number of single-parent families, the need for having both parents working outside of the home, and the stress from poverty or busy schedules, to name just a few. To make things even worse, many parents don't have a network of relatives or friends nearby to help them cope with the challenges of raising children. On the brighter side, we know a lot more about how to raise happy, well-adjusted children than we once did. Clearly, it's time to take a good look at your parenting resources and make informed decisions about the way you want to raise your children.

Examining Your Approach

In this section we'll discuss several of the factors that influence the way you approach parenting. Undoubtedly, you are doing many things well, but there's always room for improvement. Keep an open mind as you read this material; the goal is to help you discover some valuable insights about your style of parenting. Whether you should act on these insights and try to make changes is up to you.

My Parents, Myself, My Child

It's true—we tend to raise our children the same way we were raised by our parents because it feels comfortable and familiar.* This inclination has its advantages and disadvantages. One of the advantages is that it gives us a starting point for our own parenting practices. You probably know more about raising children than you think. If your childhood experiences were generally positive, you can consider it a gift from the past. Even in the best of circumstances, however, your parents made some mistakes that you don't want to repeat with your children. Changing these automatic patterns is difficult, however, because they are *habits,* like the way you comb your hair or drive your car.

Reading this book is an excellent beginning. Identifying your strengths and weaknesses is the next, critical step. You have a chance to change the patterns of parenting that have been passed down in your family for generations by making *active decisions* about these issues now, while your children are still young. Not only will your children benefit from your efforts, but their children as well.

Were your parents fair and evenhanded or moody and irritable? Did they let you get away with too much or sternly keep you under their thumb? How has their parenting influenced you? What strengths and weaknesses are you bringing with you to the job of parenting? The home practice activity for this chapter will help you make active decisions about the way you want to raise your children.

---

*Scot's note: I get that déjà vu feeling when I hear myself giving my children the same lectures my parents gave me as a child. Some of these speeches have become clichés because the situations are universal to parenting. As a joke, I finally decided to give a number to the speeches I use often so I can just say, "Speech number 53: Life isn't fair." Perhaps this, too, will become part of the family legacy.

Keeping a Positive Outlook

After a stressful day at work, your children's requests for time and attention may feel like one more demand on you. At times like this, it's easy to lose sight of the positive aspects of parenting. For obvious reasons, it's important not to become angry and irritable with your children. In this section we will discuss some ways to maintain a positive outlook on your job as a parent.

Positive Reframing

In many cases, you simply don't have much control over the events that occur in family life. Perhaps your little girl gets into a fight on the playground and you get a call from the principal's office, or the dog tears up your little boy's favorite stuffed teddy bear. What you *do* have control over is how you react to these events. Getting irritable or angry just creates a type of "social smog" that hangs over everyone in the household. Venting your frustration on other family members is the worst thing you could do because you end up hurting the very people who could give you the love and support you need.

Positive reframing is a useful technique in these situations. It involves looking for other, more constructive ways to interpret a particular situation. Sometimes this requires a bit of creativity. Suppose that your three-year-old daughter runs across the room and hits the cat with the remote control for the VCR. You've told her countless times not to hit the cat, and yet there she goes again! You immediately tell her to stop hitting the cat, and you feel like launching into an angry tirade but manage to stop yourself. How can you possibly think about this situation in a more positive way? One possibility is to focus on the fact that she is interested in the cat but doesn't know how to play appropriately with it. Reframing the situation in this way helps you feel less angry, and it leads to a constructive course of action: teaching her how to play nicely with the cat. You redirect her attention by asking her to help you find some paper and a piece of string to make a pull-toy for the cat; after you tie the paper to the string, you can show her how to play happily with the cat.

Reading negative intentions into your child's actions increases the likelihood that you will overreact to the situation (for example, thinking "He knows better than that—he did that to make me angry"). When parents of out-of-control children come in for family therapy, they are typically angry and discouraged. Even for the most disruptive kids, however, research has shown that *only 5 to 10 percent of their behavior is negative.* The first task for the therapist is to help these parents see something good about their child to build on. It could be something as small as the fact that the child is great about taking care of his tricycle: He always puts it away in the garage. By focusing on this behavior and giving him attention and praise for it, his parents can begin the process of change.

Managing Your Negative Emotions

Clearly, parents need a variety of effective techniques to help them calm down when they are dealing with child-related issues. We have already discussed one: reframing the situation and not letting yourself get caught up in thinking that the child is trying to make you angry. Remember: *You can't teach your child self-control unless you learn to control yourself.*

The old technique of silently counting to 10 when you are angry also works well. Don't feel that you have to respond right away, especially when you are upset. Tell the child to go to her room and say that you will talk to her about the situation in 5 or 10 minutes. Talk to your partner or call a friend if you think that will help. Whatever you do, don't give your child the message that she is a bad person. Try to view the problem as something that is separate from the child.

Nurturing Yourself

Don't forget to nurture yourself! Sometimes it helps to think about how lucky you are to be a parent. Coming home after a long day and having your children greet you at the door with hugs and big smiles is priceless. It also helps to think about the important work you are doing as a parent. Raising children is a challenging job. It takes love, patience, and the ability to put someone else's needs before your own. You deserve some credit for what you are doing well.

• • • • • • • • • • •

Home Practice Activity

Basic Skill (Time required: 10 minutes)
Think about the way you were raised as a child. Use the following list to describe your parents' approach to child rearing. For each category, draw an "X" through the number that best describes your mother, circle the number that describes your father, and draw an arrow to indicate the type of parent you would like to be.

Permissive									Controlling
1	2	3	4	5	6	7	8	9	10

Warm/affectionate									Cold/distant
1	2	3	4	5	6	7	8	9	10

Lots of quality time together						No quality time together			
1	2	3	4	5	6	7	8	9	10

Accepting/encouraging							Critical/discouraging		
1	2	3	4	5	6	7	8	9	10

Consistent/even tempered							Inconsistent/moody		
1	2	3	4	5	6	7	8	9	10

Physical punishment (slapping, spanking)						Nonphysical punishment (lectures, scolding)			
1	2	3	4	5	6	7	8	9	10

Playful									Serious
1	2	3	4	5	6	7	8	9	10

Good listening skills							Poor listening skills		
1	2	3	4	5	6	7	8	9	10

CHAPTER ONE

Focusing on Key Events

The scene. Dad is sitting on the couch, reading a bedtime story to his two-year-old daughter, Julia. Suddenly, his four-year-old son, Brian, runs through the living room, setting a new speed record while hanging on to the dog by the collar. Dad looks up from his book and asks Brian to please walk in the house. When Brian ignores his request, Dad starts to get up and Julia begins to whine because her reading time has been interrupted. Feeling overwhelmed, Dad sits down to finish the story as the noise level builds in the next room.

Parents are faced with scenes like this every day as they struggle to find a balance in their efforts to take care of their children's needs, spend quality time with them, and handle routine problems. Living with toddlers and young children is like standing in the middle of a three-ring circus—there's so much going on, you can't possibly pay attention to everything. The purpose of this chapter is to help you identify and respond effectively to key events within the household big top.

Family Learning Is a Two-Way Street

Parents and children learn from one another. The way parents respond to children—giving attention, ignoring, playing, scolding, and so on—teaches children whether a particular behavior is acceptable in a given situation. This is a relatively simple idea. What makes it a little more complicated is that *the learning process is a two-way street.* The way children respond to their parents—cooperating, laughing, crying, not minding, and so on—also teaches parents how to take care of their children's physical and emotional needs. Whether your child is playing with you, talking to you about the events of the day, or misbehaving in a distant corner of the house, you are both learning something.

You may have noticed that the term *learning* is being used differently here. Basically, the type of learning we are talking about concerns *small changes* produced by daily interactions in the way parents and children relate to one another. These changes are so tiny and so gradual that you may not notice them for a long time, unless you know what to look for. It's important to notice these changes because they can make a big difference over the long run. The opportunities for this type of learning are the focus of this book: They are key events within the household whirlwind. Let's see how this works in the following example.

The scene. Mom and her three-year-old son, Mike, are in the grocery store doing some shopping, when Mom's little "helper" sees a toy that he really wants.

Mike: (pointing at the toy) Mommy, can I have a squirt gun?

Mom: No, Mike, not this time.

Mike: (whining) Pleezzze, Mommy, I *want* it. My friend has a squirt gun and I need one, too. (As Mom pushes the shopping cart past the toy display, Mike sits down on the floor and begins to cry loudly.)

Mom: (In desperation, Mom grabs the squirt gun and quickly puts it in the shopping cart.) Okay, but nothing else for you today! (Mike immediately stops crying as he stands up and walks over to the shopping cart.)

What did Mom and Mike learn in this example? Mike found out that he can get what he wants by whining and crying. Mom learned that Mike will stop whining and crying (which is what she wants) when she gives in to his demands. One of the ways children gradually become uncooperative is that they learn to be *coercive* instead; that is, they learn to use unpleasant behaviors to get what they want. Although Mike's tantrum may not seem like something to be very concerned about, this behavior can develop into a more serious pattern if left unattended.

At first it may appear that it was a good idea to give Mike the squirt gun because both the mother and son got what they wanted. It's only when we look at the *long-term effect* of this exchange that we can see the problem. The next time Mom is in the store, Mike is even more likely to whine and cry when he sees something he wants because this behavior worked last time. And Mom will probably give in—perhaps more quickly this time—to keep Mike from making a scene. What are Mom and Mike learning? *In effect, Mom is teaching Mike to whine and cry, and Mike is teaching Mom to give in to his demands.* If this scene is repeated a few more times, Mike will become more demanding, and Mom will have to learn to handle the problem in another way.

Parents Are Teachers

Although family learning is a two-way street, it's up to parents to assume the role of teacher and guide the learning process. In the previous example, Mike was simply trying to achieve a short-term goal of getting the squirt gun he saw in the store. He isn't trying to become a demanding, out-of-control child, but that's what will happen if his mother doesn't take steps to teach cooperation. It may be tempting to give in to your child's demands, especially when you are tired or under a lot of stress, but it's your job to consider what this will teach your child over the long run. Teaching children self-control is hard work, but it's well worth the effort.

A good teacher consistently gives children attention and praise for their efforts and good behavior, and ignores or sets limits on children's misbehavior. Giving children attention and praise for good behavior sets the stage for cooperation, and the positive feeling you put into the message makes it even more powerful. On the other hand, when you set limits on children's misbehavior, it's important to do it without being irritable or angry. This means that you have to learn to control *your own* emotions to be an effective teacher. (Some useful techniques for managing your emotions were presented in the Introduction.)

For the most part, it's up to parents to make their own decisions about how they want their children to behave. For example, some parents don't seem to care about whining but are concerned when their children won't mind, and teaching children good table manners is more important to some parents than it is to others. Parents should follow their personal preferences in making decisions about these issues. There are, however, some generally accepted limits. Most parents would agree that extreme behaviors, such as stealing, hitting, and cruelty to animals, just aren't permissible. But within reasonable limits, parents have a broad range of choices regarding how they want their children to behave.

Double Trouble for Mom

I don't know how many times I've told you not to leave your things in the living room. Just look at this mess! You two aren't going anywhere until you help me pick up your stuff!

Paying Attention to Details

One of the basic requirements of effective parenting is to stay close to the action and pay attention to details. Are your children good about sharing, or do they often fight over toys? When does your toddler whine, and how do other family members respond when this happens? These are key events for parents. If parents are distant and uninvolved, they cannot guide and supervise their children. When parents fail to take this responsibility, the social development of their children is left to chance.

Before you can start making changes, you need to pay careful attention to what your child is doing *now*. One of the best ways to focus your attention is to define the child's behavior in specific terms and count how often it occurs. This process is important for three reasons. First, it will help you discover whether a particular behavior really is a problem. You may find, for example, that your child doesn't whine as often as you thought. Second, if you know how often a particular behavior happens now, you will be able to tell whether the approach you are using is having an effect on the child's behavior. Third, and perhaps most important, you will discover what *you* are doing that contributes to the problem.

Three of the most common problem behaviors in young children are temper tantrums, whining, and not minding. Let's practice defining these behaviors in specific terms. A temper tantrum usually consists of a flurry of out-of-control behaviors such as screaming, hitting, and perhaps lying on the floor, kicking and thrashing. A good definition for whining would be talking in a high-pitched, annoying, childish tone of voice. Not minding means that the child doesn't cooperate with a request right away (within 10 or 15 seconds) the first time the request is made. Think about these definitions. Are they specific enough that most parents would be able to recognize the behaviors in their own children? How would you change these definitions to make them fit your child better?

The positive behaviors most parents want to foster in young children include playing quietly, sharing, taking turns, helping with household duties, and being polite. Looking for good behavior is important because it helps you appreciate what your child is doing right. Think about how you would define your child's positive behaviors in specific terms. For example, what does being polite mean? Your list would include things like saying hello when you are introduced to someone, not interrupting when someone else is talking, and saying please and thank you.

Watching Carefully

The home practice activity for this chapter is to keep track of one or two things your child is doing now. The first step in this activity is to define a behavior that you would like to have more information about. The following is a list of typical behaviors that concern parents with young children.

Common Label	More Specific Definition
out of control	has temper tantrums, won't accept "no"
messy	doesn't put toys away
selfish	doesn't share toys with playmates
uncooperative	doesn't mind requests within 15 seconds
aggressive	hits, bites, pushes, threatens
courteous	asks nicely, says please and thank you
caring	shows concern for the feelings of others

Note that this list includes both positive and problem behaviors and that the *definition* of a problem behavior is often much more neutral than the common *label* for it. Negative labels such as "brat" are often harmful because they offer little hope for improvement. Because the definition of a behavior is more specific, it's more useful in that it provides information that will help you identify the key events for this behavior. This is the foundation for helping your child change.

The goal is to describe what you see your child doing in terms that anyone could understand. This is called the *stranger rule*. Your definition should be clear enough that a stranger visiting in your home could easily recognize the behavior. For example, does having a "good attitude" mean smiling, cooperating with requests, being helpful, or asking nicely? In this example, it would be better to track each of these components separately. If we think of this in terms of our previous discussion, the phrase "good attitude" is the common label, and the components are the more specific definition.

Once you have a clear definition of the child's behavior, the next step is to count how often you see it. To do this, pick the time of day that the behavior occurs most often—for example, during morning routines, in the hour just before dinner, and during transitions such as going to school. These are often difficult times for families. There are many key events during these periods, which means there are many opportunities for family learning and changing behavior. These are good times to track a specific behavior.

Summary

We have discussed several important ideas in this chapter. The first is that family learning is a two-way street. When you spend time with your child, you are both learning something—that is, you are producing small changes in each other's behavior. The important point is that it's up to parents to guide the learning process, which means that parents must be able to identify key events within the household and know how to respond effectively to them.

The role of key events in family learning is a topic we will discuss throughout this book. We have briefly introduced the idea that parents must consider both the short-term and long-term consequences of key events to understand the impact those events have on family learning. The example of Mom and Mike in the grocery store was used to illustrate this point.

Another related idea is that parents are teachers. Like any good teacher, parents must be involved in what their children are doing to be effective. This means dealing with problems that arise and not taking children's positive behaviors for granted. *These are key events that deserve your attention.*

One of the parenting practices that will help you stay focused on key events is to define your child's behaviors (both positive and negative) in specific terms instead of using common labels, which are often negative and harmful. The *stranger rule* requires that your definition is clear enough that a stranger would be able to understand what you mean.

. . . .

Home Practice Activity

Basic Skill (Time required: 10 minutes)
Focus on one of your child's behaviors that you are concerned about. Try to pick a behavior that you see fairly often. Several examples include fussy eating, refusing to share toys, whining, hitting, not minding, not going to bed, or bad table manners. If you don't have any concerns right now, focus on cooperation.

Write the common label and a more specific definition of the behavior on the following form. Then have someone read the definition and make sure he or she understands what it means. If necessary, write a new definition.

The common label for the behavior is _____.

The specific definition of the behavior is _____

_____

_____

_____.

Did someone read your definition?   Yes ❑   No ❑

If you think you can improve on your first definition—based either on what you have observed (your child's behavior) or on the feedback you received from the person who read your definition—write a new definition. _____

_____

_____

Advanced Skill (Time required: 60 minutes)
Think about the time of day that you usually see the behavior you have selected (for example, at dinner time, when your child is getting ready for school, or during play time). For the next four days, spend at least 10 to 15 minutes doing some careful watching and record keeping at this time of day. *Fill out the record-keeping form every time you see the*

behavior. If your child asks what you're doing, say that you're trying to learn more about the family.

Let's look at a form that has been filled out to see how this works.

Record-Keeping Form

Day 1	Behavior: Whining	
Situation	*Family members' response*	*(Optional)* *Outcome: child did or didn't get his/her way*
① at store	Ⓐor I	⊕or –
② with blocks	Ⓐor I	+ orⒸ
③ snack	A or Ⓘ	+ orⒸ
④ TV show	A or Ⓘ	+ orⒸ
⑤ bedtime	A or Ⓘ	+ orⒸ

Directions: Every time you see the behavior, circle the next number on the left of the form. A word or two can be used to identify any situation, as shown in this example. In the middle column, circle the letter that indicates whether the reaction of family members was ignore (I) or attend (A). Ignore means that the child's behavior was *completely* ignored by everyone. Examples of attend include any response from anyone: saying something (even scolding), gesturing with hands or facial expressions, and physical contact (touching/holding).

Optional: Circle the plus or minus sign in the right column of the form to show the outcome of the child's behavior: Did the child get his or her way, or was the behavior unsuccessful from the child's point of view?

Looking back at this record-keeping form, notice that the child only received attention twice for misbehavior and a positive outcome just once. The family members in this example are doing a reasonably good job of ignoring the child's misbehavior and not letting the child get his or her way as a reward for problem behavior. Even so, it would be worthwhile for this family to work on giving the child less attention for misbehavior.

Record-Keeping Form

Day 1   Behavior:

Situation	Family members' response	*(Optional)* Outcome: child did or didn't get his/her way
1	A or I	+ or −
2	A or I	+ or −
3	A or I	+ or −
4	A or I	+ or −
5	A or I	+ or −

Record-Keeping Form

Day 2   Behavior:

Situation	Family members' response	*(Optional)* Outcome: child did or didn't get his/her way
1	A or I	+ or −
2	A or I	+ or −
3	A or I	+ or −
4	A or I	+ or −
5	A or I	+ or −

Record-Keeping Form

Day 3   Behavior:

Situation	Family members' response	(Optional) Outcome: child did or didn't get his/her way
1	A or I	+ or −
2	A or I	+ or −
3	A or I	+ or −
4	A or I	+ or −
5	A or I	+ or −

Record-Keeping Form

Day 4   Behavior:

Situation	Family members' response	(Optional) Outcome: child did or didn't get his/her way
1	A or I	+ or −
2	A or I	+ or −
3	A or I	+ or −
4	A or I	+ or −
5	A or I	+ or −

Record-Keeping Form

Day 5		Behavior:	

Situation	Family members' response	(Optional) Outcome: child did or didn't get his/her way
1	A or I	+ or −
2	A or I	+ or −
3	A or I	+ or −
4	A or I	+ or −
5	A or I	+ or −

Record-Keeping Form

Day 6		Behavior:	

Situation	Family members' response	(Optional) Outcome: child did or didn't get his/her way
1	A or I	+ or −
2	A or I	+ or −
3	A or I	+ or −
4	A or I	+ or −
5	A or I	+ or −

CHAPTER TWO

....

Teaching Cooperation

The scene. Dad and his three-year-old daughter, Christy, are playing with building blocks in the living room. Now it's time to put the blocks away.

Dad: It's time to clean up, Christy. I'll need some help picking up the blocks and putting them in the bucket.

Christy: (She slowly puts a few blocks away and then gets distracted.)

Dad: It looks like we have a few more blocks left. Hey, I'll bet I can put more of these in the bucket than you can. Ready, set, go!

Christy: (Looking up at her dad, Christy smiles as she grabs a handful of blocks and quickly puts them in the bucket.) I'm good at putting these away, Dad. Watch me.

Dad: (He laughs and slowly puts blocks into the bucket as he watches Christy.) You're just too fast for me! Maybe I'll be able to keep up with you next time.

Christy: (She looks pleased as she puts the lid on the bucket.) All done! (claps her hands)

Dad: Good job!

It's important to get your relationship with toddlers and young children off to a good start by promoting cooperation. In this example, Dad wanted Christy to cooperate with his request to help with the building blocks. He clearly stated what he wanted, and then he challenged Christy to a race to maintain her interest. Finally, he let her "win" and commented on her success. This is a very powerful approach to use with young children; they love the idea that they can do something better than their parents.

It's also helpful to establish routines for daily tasks such as putting toys away, putting dirty dishes in the sink, hanging up coats, and so on. The earlier you start developing routines and the more consistent you are, the less trouble you will have getting children to do these simple tasks without nagging.* This approach reduces the risk of getting into power struggles, and it encourages cooperation.

Learning to cooperate with requests, sharing, taking turns when talking, and caring for the feelings of others are relatively high-level skills that toddlers and young children must develop to get along with others and make friends. As we will see in the next several chapters, these skills are learned during play and by watching and interacting with others.

There are enormous long-term benefits for children who know how to be cooperative and attentive. Cooperative children are usually well-liked by their peers and adults, and people enjoy participating in activities with them and helping them improve their skills. Uncooperative children, on the other hand, are often rejected by their peers because of their unpleasant behavior, and they tend to have low self-esteem and problems in school. As these children grow older, they often become defiant and aggressive, and during the teenage years they are at risk for more serious problem behaviors. Clearly, your efforts to develop a cooperative relationship with your child is very important work. In the next section we'll discuss the role that parental requests play in promoting cooperation.

Tom's note: One of the routines we adopted in our family was that the children had to be dressed and ready for school in the morning before they could eat breakfast or watch TV. This approach made the morning routine much easier for everyone.

Using Requests Effectively

Teaching children to cooperate with routine requests is a key issue for parents. It's at the heart of most behavior problems in children. Studies have shown that the approach parents use when making requests is critical because it sets the stage for cooperation. Let's take a look at how this works.

Basically, there are two types of requests. Some requests are attempts to get children to *do* something, such as picking up their toys. Other requests (or commands) are intended to *stop* children from doing something, such as hitting the dog. In either case, parents clearly want their children's cooperation. If children ignore requests, parents often make one of the following mistakes: They either nag their children or let it go. Nagging puts parents in the unpleasant position of badgering and gives children attention for being uncooperative. Letting it go, on the other hand, teaches children that it isn't necessary to take their parents' requests seriously.

Planning for Success

It takes planning to use requests effectively. Think about how you feel when people ask you to do something—their approach makes all the difference. For the same reason, you need to develop a plan for using requests that works. Your plan should include the four points that follow. As you review each of these points, think about how it applies to your child.

1. Get the child's attention. Use a firm, clear voice, and check to make sure the child is listening. Sometimes a child will distract himself by playing while you are talking; when this happens, try touching the child on the arm and make sure you have good eye contact. If the child is watching a show on TV instead of listening to you, stand in front of the TV.

2. Give a prompt. A prompt, which is advance warning of a request, will help your child get ready to shift gears and change her activity. If your five-year-old daughter is playing in the bathtub, for example, give her a warning that it will be time to get out of the tub in five minutes. A younger child doesn't understand what five minutes means, so you would simply say that it's almost time to get out of the bathtub. When you give a prompt, don't get into an argument with the child; keep it short and to the point.

3. Use good timing. Take into account what your child is doing. No one likes to be interrupted while doing something fun like playing. If your child is drawing a picture, for example, wait to make the request until he is almost done. Again, this would be a good time to give a prompt so the child knows what to expect: "You can work on your picture for five more minutes, Todd; then it's time to get ready for bed."

4. Don't make requests too often. Being bombarded by requests from parents is overwhelming for children, and it leads to power struggles. Save your requests for important things, and only make requests that you intend to enforce. Try to limit yourself to 10 or 15 requests per day. This means that *minor events should be ignored.* For example, if your child is humming a nursery song over and over and it begins to bother you, think before you ask the child to stop. Is this request important? Can I get the child to stop by using a distraction instead? There is a good chance that the child will soon become bored with the rhyme and stop humming without any prompting. One of the home practice exercises for this chapter is to keep track of how often you use requests and commands and to think about which ones are necessary.

The Five Essential Rules for Making Requests

The four points just discussed will get you off to a good start, but the way you actually make the request is equally important. In this section we discuss the five basic rules for making good requests. Let's discuss these one at a time.

1. Be pleasant. Pay attention to the tone of voice you use when you ask your child to do something. Try to be pleasant when making requests, even

One More Request to Save the Cat

I know I shouldn't ignore this, but I've already made 10 requests today . . .

if you're upset with something your child has (or hasn't) done. It may help to imagine that you are talking to an adult friend or someone you admire. Watch your tone of voice—if you're irritable or angry, it just makes a bad situation worse. Also, don't get into the habit of bringing up past failures or giving the child a lecture. Focus on your goal, which is to have the child cooperate with your request. Avoid criticizing or blaming your child when making requests. Comments such as "Stop being so lazy" and "Why would you do something stupid like that?" disrupt children's cooperative, positive behavior. Try to be pleasant or at least neutral, even if you have negative thoughts and feelings about the current situation.

2. Use statements. Parents often use questions when they make requests, such as, "Don't you think it's time to get out of the bathtub now?" Perhaps parents do this because they think it softens their message. The problem is that stating your request as a question gives the child an opportunity to argue or simply say no, and in most cases parents are not willing to accept either of these responses. Also, it's difficult for a child to understand what you want her to do if you use a question. If you want a child to cooperate, use a simple statement. In the previous example, it would be much better to say, "It's time to get out of the bathtub now."

3. Make one request at a time. The best way to encourage a child's cooperation is to make one request at a time, using as few words as possible. Also, make sure that you say something positive about the child's efforts to respond to each request. If you do this consistently, your child will be more likely to cooperate with your requests in the future.

Parents often make the mistake of chaining their requests together. It sounds something like this: "Jenna, it's time for bed now. I want you to turn off the TV, brush your teeth, put your jammies on, and come in here for your bedtime story. Hurry up—it's getting late!" Even under the best of circumstances, it would be very difficult for a five-year-old child to remember four requests presented at the same time. Young children easily get distracted (start playing with a favorite toy and so on) before finishing a list of tasks. Giving a chain of requests sets the child up for failure, and it sets you up to nag and make negative statements about the child's efforts.

4. Be specific. This basic rule of good communication is often overlooked by parents. For example, "Clean up your room" is too vague. It would be better to say, "Pick up your building blocks and put them in the bucket." The more specific a request is, the better. When the child has finished, look for at least one thing she did well and say something positive about it, such as, "That was fast—great job!" Then you can go on to the next thing you want her to do. It's particularly important to use this approach with toddlers and young children. As we saw in the previous example of Christy and her dad, making the task into a game is a great way to encourage cooperation.

5. Make realistic requests. If you follow the four basic rules just discussed, children will try to cooperate with your requests most of the time. Unfortunately, if you ask children to do something that is unrealistic for their age, it is impossible for them to cooperate. For example, asking a two-year-old to make his own bed is unrealistic.

It's up to you to determine which tasks you can expect your child to do. During the preschool years, each child develops skills and abilities at very different rates. As the child's parent, you are in the best position to judge what your child is capable of doing on a given day. When you are making this judgment, it's important to keep all of the circumstances in mind. For example, when your preschool child has just come home after a long, hot ride in the car, it's not a good time to make a request. We suggest that you increase your chances of success by only requesting behaviors you're sure your child can do. Sometimes this means taking a difficult chore and breaking it down into smaller, more realistic tasks. A two-year-old can help put blocks away, but asking him to clean up the playroom is too much.

Being a parent means making requests. If you practice the steps outlined in this chapter, you may be surprised at the difference it makes in your child's cooperation. In the chapters that follow, we will discuss other parenting practices that build on this important foundation.

Summary

Parents are faced with the important task of teaching cooperation during the toddler and preschool years. Doing this directly shapes several critical areas of children's development: making friends, being accepted by adults, and learning new skills. Parents can get their children off to a good start by practicing the guidelines for making requests described in this chapter. First, set the stage for cooperation by getting the child's attention, giving a prompt, using good timing, and not making requests too often. Second, follow the five essential rules for making good requests: Be pleasant, use statements (not questions), make one request at a time, be specific, and make realistic requests. This approach will reduce the time you spend yelling and nagging at your children and make it much easier to build a warm and cooperative relationship with them.

• • • • • • • • • • •

Home Practice Activity

Basic Skill (Time required: 15 minutes)
Pick a time of day when you usually make a lot of requests (for example, at dinner time or in the morning), and for 15 minutes count how often you and your partner ask your child to do something (or stop doing something); try to make at least two requests during this time.

How many requests did you make?
(circle or cross out the next number as you make requests)

1   2   3   4   5   6   7   8   9   10   11   12   13   14   15

Advanced Skill (Time required: 45 minutes)
During the next three days, spend 10 to 15 minutes keeping track of your requests. Again, choose a time of day when you usually make a lot of requests. Then pick one or two of the situations and fill out the rest of the Using Good Requests form; this exercise will help you find ways to improve your approach to making requests.

Using Good Requests

Day 1
How many requests did you make?
(circle or cross out the next number as you make requests)

1   2   3   4   5   6   7   8   9   10   11   12   13   14   15

Situation 1
Describe what your child was doing. _____
_____

Write down what you said when you made your request. _____
_____
_____
Was your request really necessary?   Yes ❑   No ❑

Did you remember to:
Get the child's attention?   Yes ❑   No ❑
Give a prompt?   Yes ❑   No ❑
Use good timing?   Yes ❑   No ❑
Be pleasant?   Yes ❑   No ❑
Use a statement (not a question)?   Yes ❑   No ❑
Make one request at a time?   Yes ❑   No ❑
Be specific?   Yes ❑   No ❑
Make sure your request was realistic?   Yes ❑   No ❑

Situation 2
Describe what your child was doing. _____
_____

Write down what you said when you made your request. _____
_____
_____
Was your request really necessary?   Yes ❑   No ❑
Did you remember to:
Get the child's attention?   Yes ❑   No ❑
Give a prompt?   Yes ❑   No ❑
Use good timing?   Yes ❑   No ❑
Be pleasant?   Yes ❑   No ❑
Use a statement (not a question)?   Yes ❑   No ❑
Make one request at a time?   Yes ❑   No ❑
Be specific?   Yes ❑   No ❑
Make sure your request was realistic?   Yes ❑   No ❑

CHAPTER THREE

....

Supporting Children's Positive Behavior

The scene. Dad is trying to get his three-year-old daughter, Melissa, ready for daycare. He's running late, as usual, but he is managing to stay calm. He still needs to put her shoes on, but he can't seem to find them.

Dad: (Kneeling down to make eye contact with Melissa, he talks to her in a pleasant tone of voice.) Melissa, I need your help. I can't seem to find your shoes. I think they're in your bedroom—please go look for them and bring them back to me.

Melissa: (looking up at him) Okay, Dad. (She smiles and walks off to find her shoes. About two minutes later, she comes back with one shoe and her favorite doll.)

Dad: (He's reading his notes for the morning meeting but looks up and smiles when he sees her coming.) Good job—it looks like you found them! Is the other shoe in there?

Melissa: (nodding her head) Uh-huh.

Dad: That's great! Go get it for me, quick like a bunny, okay?

Melissa: (Giving Dad the shoe, she darts off into her room. A few seconds later, she comes back with the other shoe. She looks up at Dad with a big smile.) Here, Daddy!

Dad: Good job, Melissa, that's a big help! (He gives her a hug and quickly puts her shoes on.) Now we're all ready to go!

This dad gets extra credit for turning a stressful situation into an opportunity to teach cooperation. Even though he was late for work, he didn't criticize Melissa or take over when she brought only one shoe. Instead, he praised her positive efforts and coaxed her to complete the task on her own by repeating his request in a playful tone of voice. When she promptly brought the second shoe, Dad praised her again and gave her a hug. Through his positive attention, Dad made it clear to Melissa that her efforts were noticed and appreciated. Both Dad and Melissa played their roles perfectly: Melissa cooperated with Dad's request (even though she did get distracted when she went to her room, which can be expected with three-year-olds), and Dad was patient and consistently supported her positive efforts.

Cooperation is like a dance. The first step is the parent's request, the second step is the child's cooperation, and the third step is the most important—*the parent's support.* Children's cooperation should not be taken for granted; your positive attention provides the incentive for your children to join you in the dance.

Giving Children Incentives

Toddlers and preschoolers will endlessly repeat behaviors that receive positive responses, such as attention, hugs, and praise, from the people around them. These reactions provide powerful incentives for the child's behavior. In this chapter we will see how young children are strongly influenced by the positive reactions of their parents, siblings, and friends.

An incentive is anything that can be used to strengthen children's behavior. Although the only incentives we have discussed so far are positive reactions from people, the list also includes colorful stickers, additional privileges (for example, having a friend come over), money, special time with a parent, a favorite dessert, and doing a project together. Once you get the hang of it, the only limit to thinking up new incentives is your imagination!

The effect that incentives have on behavior is called *positive reinforcement*. Behaviors that receive positive reinforcement are strengthened, which means that children will repeat them more often. Whether you're aware of it or not, positive reinforcement is constantly at work shaping the character of your child. Praising a child for sharing a toy or hugging a child who is having a tantrum has the same effect: In each case, the child's behavior (sharing or having a tantrum) is reinforced or strengthened.

Using incentives to encourage children's positive behavior is a basic building block of good parenting. It promotes children's self-confidence and prevents problem behaviors at the same time. *When children receive attention for positive behavior, they are less likely to misbehave to get attention.*

The trick to using incentives successfully is to "catch" your children being good. Parents often get into the habit of doing just the opposite; they only seem to notice when their children are misbehaving, and they jump in to correct them. This chapter will show you how to use incentives to bring out the best in your children. We want you to give special attention to your children's positive behavior: for example, playing quietly, being gentle with the cat, offering to help (even if it's inconvenient for you at the time), brushing their teeth, saying hello when they are introduced to someone, sharing playthings, and cooperating with your requests. These are behaviors that all parents appreciate but tend to take for granted.

The PIE Recipe for Incentives

Studies have shown that effective incentives have the following characteristics: They are Pleasant for the child, they are given Immediately after the behavior, and they are given Every time the behavior occurs. Notice that the first letters of these important ingredients for success spell "PIE." This is not the kind of pie that grandmother used to make, but it's still a treat the whole family can enjoy. When parents say, "I've already tried using incentives and it didn't work," it's usually because they overlooked one or more ingredients in the PIE recipe. As we discuss each ingredient, think about your own style of parenting. How do you respond to your children's positive behavior?

A Reward for Maria

Well, Maria, since you ate all of your lunch, we've decided to give you a special treat!

Incentives work because they are reinforcing, which means that they are things that are *pleasant for the child*. Typically, a good incentive is something the child enjoys or wants. Certain incentives seem to work with most children: a hug from Mom or Dad, a special treat, praise, or perhaps a colorful sticker. Other incentives depend on the individual child. Looking for rocks with Mom may be a powerful incentive for one child, while another child might prefer having Dad read a special story.

To find incentives that will work with your child, think about your child's particular interests and the things that other children the same age enjoy. It's a lot like buying a birthday present—you have to think about your child's hobbies, interests, and personality to make good choices; the difference is that in this case you are looking for small things you can give every day. When in doubt, ask your child. Also, many of the activities your child may currently take for granted, such as watching television or going to the park, can be used as incentives. Part of the home practice activity for this chapter is to create a list of incentives that you can use with your child.

To be reinforcing, incentives also need to be given *immediately* after the positive behavior. With young children in particular, the sooner you give the incentive, the better it will work. The goal is to help the child recognize the connection between her positive behavior and receiving the reward. The best approach is to use *small* incentives that you can give right away; positive attention, praise, and hugs are good choices. Stickers and special treats are also fun for toddlers and preschoolers, and they can be given to the child without interrupting his play.

Incentives are most effective if they are given to the child every time you see a particular behavior, at least for a while. *If you want results, you have to be consistent.* Again, this helps children make the connection between their positive behavior and receiving the incentive. For example, if you want to teach your little girl to share her toys, focus on that behavior for a few days and give her lots of positive attention every time you see her share. At first you may have to prompt her by saying something like "Remember to share your toys." Every time she does, praise her for her positive behavior: "I'm really proud of you for doing such a good job of sharing!"

The following scene illustrates how the PIE recipe works.

The scene. Mom is shopping for groceries with her five-year-old son, Matthew. As they walk into the store, Matthew notices a toy-dispensing machine with colorful trinkets in it.

Matthew: (pointing to the machine) Mom! Can I have a quarter so I can get one of these?

Mom: No, Matthew, not now. We're here to shop for groceries, not to buy more toys. (She turns away and grabs a shopping cart.)

Matthew: But, Mom, I'll pay you back with my allowance. It's only a quarter. *Dad* always buys me something. (He starts to look upset.)

Mom: I'll tell you what. If you do a good job of helping me with the shopping, with no complaining, I'll give you a quarter. Is that a deal? (Matthew looks up and nods in agreement. All goes well until about five minutes later . . .)

Matthew: Mom, how much longer? My legs are getting tired.

Mom: (matter-of-factly) We're about halfway done. You remember our deal, don't you? You've done a great job so far, and all you have to do is keep it up for a few more minutes and you'll get the quarter I promised you.

Matthew: O-o-o-kay. (He looks bored, but stops complaining.)

Mom: (When they get to the checkout stand, Mom reaches into her pocket and gives Matthew a quarter.) Thanks for being such a good shopper! Here's your quarter. (Matthew looks pleased as he rushes off to get his prize.)

In this scene, Mom quickly recognized that she could use the quarter Matthew wanted as an incentive to make the shopping experience go smoothly. When Matthew slipped into his usual pattern of complaining, all it took was one reminder from Mom, and Matthew corrected his behavior. When the shopping was over, Mom immediately gave Matthew his reward and commented on his good effort. Because Matthew had asked for the quarter, Mom already knew it would be pleasant (reinforcing) for him. Also notice that Mom ignored Matthew's attempt to sidetrack the issue ("Dad always buys me something"). If she had gotten caught up in a discussion about what Dad does, she might have missed the opportunity to help Matthew learn to be cooperative during shopping trips.

Here's another variation on this technique. In this case, the child asks Mom to buy a Twinkie when they first enter the grocery store. Mom tells him that for each aisle they go down, he can earn one letter of the word "Twinkie" if he is well behaved all the way down the aisle. If he earns all of the letters, he gets the Twinkie. This is an effective approach with slightly older children for several reasons: It breaks the goal into smaller steps (earning one letter for each aisle), it gives the child a chance to make some mistakes (with immediate feedback) and still earn the reward, and it's also good spelling practice!

Helpful Hints

In addition to the PIE recipe, there are several other things to keep in mind when you are using incentives. Remember to reward the *small steps* that a young child must take to learn the complete behavior. For example, it will take several steps over a period of several months to teach a toddler to put away his toys. At first, reward him for *any* positive efforts (this was illustrated in the scene at the beginning of this chapter), even for putting away a single toy if he's cooperative. The trick is to look for positive behavior to build on. Once he is a little older and doing well with the first step, reward him for taking slightly larger steps, such as putting away several toys without complaining. When he has developed the habit of putting his toys away, you can gradually *fade out* the use of incentives for this behavior and start working on something else. It's best to focus on just one or two behaviors at a time. Also, keep in mind that you will probably have to give him a "tune up" on putting away toys from time to time to keep him on track.

In the next section we'll discuss a key issue for many families: how incentives can be used to improve daily routines.

Improving Daily Routines

The scene. Evenings in the Gonzales household can be hectic, especially when the neighborhood kids come over to play. It's dinner time, and Dad is trying to get four-year-old Maria and five-year-old Roberto to pick up their toys before coming to the table for dinner.

> **Dad:** (Walking into the living room, he sees toys scattered all over the floor.) Maria and Roberto, it's almost dinner time, and I want you to pick up all of these toys now.

> **Roberto:** (briefly looking up from his play activity) Okay, Dad. In a minute.

(Dad turns and walks into the kitchen to help Mom put dinner on the table. Meanwhile, Roberto and Maria put some of the toys away but soon become distracted and begin playing again with their friends. A few minutes later, Dad walks back into the living room and sees that the kids are involved in a new activity.)

> **Dad:** (in an angry tone) What's going on here? I thought I told you guys to put the toys away. (sighs) Look, dinner is getting cold, so let's eat. But I expect you to pick up the toys after dinner. Is

that a deal? (Roberto and Maria nod in agreement, say good-bye to their friends, and run happily into the dining room.)

We all know what's going to happen after dinner—there's a good chance Dad will forget to follow through with his request for Maria and Roberto to pick up their toys. In the end, Mom or Dad will probably put the toys away. What do you think will happen the next time Dad asks the kids to pick up their toys? Roberto and Maria are very likely to politely ignore him because that has worked in the past. Eventually, Dad may become frustrated and resort to other tactics, such as yelling.

In the long run, it would have been better for Dad to put dinner on hold for five minutes while he helped the kids pick up their toys (which is better than doing it all himself!). Then he could have reinforced them for cooperating by saying, "Thanks for the help! Let's go wash up and have some dinner." Since the children are looking forward to eating dinner, this is also an incentive for their appropriate behavior. The goal is to look beyond the immediate situation (dinner is getting cold) to find opportunities that will allow you to support children's positive efforts.

Be Prepared

Daily routines are part of every household. When you have small children, every transition—from making sure the children have brushed their teeth to getting everyone in the car—can be a trying experience. Using incentives is a good way to help children make transitions smoothly. Be prepared by making a list of things that your child wants or enjoys so you will be able to select a suitable reward when an opportunity arises. Remember: Incentives don't have to be something that you buy, although a grab bag of small items can be useful. A hug, some words of praise, a bubble bath, or a special bedtime story are excellent choices.

Issues in Using Incentives

Some parents object to the idea of using incentives and rewards to guide children's behavior. We will briefly discuss three of the main issues that parents are often concerned about.

Are Incentives Bribes?

Some parents think that incentives are bribes. After all, why should you have to give children a reward for doing something they should just do on their own? Isn't that bribery? Although these are valid concerns, there are some good reasons to change your thinking about using incentives. First, it's up to parents to teach their young children to be responsible through many small steps, and incentives are an important part of that learning process. To expect young children to take care of themselves without support from their parents is unrealistic. Second, a bribe is different from a reward in that a bribe is used to make someone do something dishonest or unethical. Teaching your child to go to bed without a fuss is not dishonest or unethical. Also, a bribe is usually given before the behavior is performed, but an incentive should be given after the behavior has occurred. For example, saying, "You can have your dessert now if you promise to eat your dinner afterwards" is using dessert as a bribe, but saying, "You can have dessert after you eat your dinner" is using dessert as a reward. Keep in mind that parents provide incentives for children every day. What we are suggesting is that parents use them productively to teach positive behavior and prevent problems. It's simply a matter of good timing.

Do Children Become Reward Dependent?

Another concern that parents often have about using incentives is that children will learn to withhold good behavior unless they receive a reward. This can be a problem when children are older (around age six or seven) and become concerned with understanding rules and issues of fairness. When they reach this age, you may hear, "What will I get if I do that?"

You can prevent this problem by discreetly weaving incentives into the course of daily living without drawing too much attention to the fact that you are supporting positive behavior. Be consistent in reinforcing the one or two behaviors you specifically want to support, and at the same time surprise your children with special incentives for their good behavior. On a Saturday morning, for example, you might say, "You guys have been great all morning—let's go see that new movie, okay?"

As each new positive behavior is strengthened, you will gradually reduce the use of incentives for that behavior and move on to something else. Children enjoy learning new skills and taking more responsibility for themselves if the steps are manageable. As children grow older, they also become more independent. Contributing to the household makes them feel important and worthwhile. Rules like "Make your bed before you go out to play" teach them good work habits. In the long run, everyone wins when incentives are used properly—the parents, the child, and everyone else in the family.

How Do Love and Nurturing Fit In?

One of the questions that often comes up about incentives is how they fit in with the love and attention that parents normally give their children. Should parents give warmth and love to children *only as incentives for good behavior?* The answer is that no, parents should show that they care about their children with lots of hugs, love, and attention—the more you give a child, the better—*just make sure the child isn't misbehaving when you do it.* Parental nurturing makes the world comfortable and secure for children. Incentives such as hugs, praise, and attention do not have to be withheld to be powerful incentives for children. (If children receive too many privileges, however, they will stop working as incentives.) The balancing act for parents is to give their children plenty of love throughout the day, but also to keep in mind *what their children are learning from their responses.* Does this sound like a big job? It is, but it's also an important one!

Summary

When parents use incentives effectively, they provide support for children's positive efforts, gently guide their development, and prevent misbehavior. It's fun to catch your children being good and to come up with new ways to reward their small successes. This approach builds children's self-esteem and self-confidence. Children thrive on attention, hugs, and praise. Stickers, special privileges, and treats are nice, too. As long as you use these incentives correctly, there is no way to overdo it!

Both you and your child will feel good about the shift toward more positive exchanges.

Most parents already use incentives, but they are often inconsistent about it. Incentives are most effective when parents follow the PIE recipe. The reward or incentive should be *pleasant* to the child, and it should be given *immediately, every time* the behavior occurs.

Incentives also help family routines, such as getting ready for dinner or going to school, go more smoothly. Families with young children often run into problems during these transitions. Again, the key is to use incentives to support your child's cooperation with these routines.

• • • • • • • • • • •

Home Practice Activity

Basic Skill (Time required: 10 minutes)
Make a list of incentives that you could give your child at a moment's notice: a hug, praise, a fun activity, a treat, a grab bag of small toys, or activities that are readily available (for example, a special videotape). A form is provided to help you create a list. Be sure to make a list for each child so that you can take his or her interests into account. What are some simple things that your child enjoys?

List of Incentives
Child's name _____

1. _____

2. _____

3. _____

4. _____

5. _____

List of Incentives
Child's name _____

1. _____

2. _____

3. _____

4. _____

5. _____

List of Incentives
Child's name _____

1. _____

2. _____

3. _____

4. _____

5. _____

Advanced Skill (Time required: 45 minutes)
The next part of your assignment is to catch your child being good.
When she cooperates with your requests, label the positive behavior
and give her one of the incentives on your list. Also, use these incentives to support other positive behaviors that you may take for granted,
such as sharing and politeness. Try to catch your child being good at
least twice each day for the next three days. Use the form on the next
page to keep track of your practice sessions. When you use an incentive
to support one of the positive behaviors listed on the form, write the incentive used in the appropriate box.

Catch Your Child Being Good

	Day 1	*Day 2*	*Day 3*
Cooperation			
Offering to help			
Politeness			
Sharing			
Independent play			
Gentleness			
Kindness			
Self-care (brushing teeth, etc.)			
Other			

CHAPTER FOUR

∙∙

Using Stickers and Star Charts

The scene. Four-year-old Kobin is all smiles as he bursts into his parents' bedroom early one morning. "Mom . . . Dad," he says excitedly, "I stayed in my bed all night!" Mom sits up in bed and beckons him to her, puts her arm around him, and yawns. "That's great, Kobin. You know what that means—another sticker on your chart! Let's go see how many you have now."

In this scene, Kobin has taken another step toward learning to stay in his own bed all night long. This can be quite an accomplishment for young children who have gotten into the habit of coming into their parents' bed when they wake up at night. Even though Kobin's parents may lose a little sleep in the morning, they know that in the long run their commitment to teaching this new behavior will lead to positive changes within the family.

In the previous chapter we talked about incentives and how they are powerful motivators that help children learn new skills and become more self-reliant. Young children need lots of support when they are trying out new skills or breaking bad habits. Stickers and star charts are the perfect answer for providing this kind of support. These charts are wonderful teaching tools—and, best of all, they are both inexpensive and easy for parents to use.

Sometimes you have to think ahead to use incentives and rewards effectively. A little planning really helps. We now turn to "tried and true" strategies that parents can use as plans for making changes in their own family.

Stickers and Stars

Stickers and star charts provide a structured approach that reminds parents to encourage children's positive efforts and to practice preventive parenting, or parenting that prevents problems. We use a plan to excel at work; why not use one to help you do a better job of parenting? What job could be more important?

We will consider several ways to use stickers and charts with children of various ages. A sticker on the hand is just as effective as a chart for toddlers and children up to the age of three or four. A simple sticker chart works best with preschoolers because it is visually oriented and doesn't require reading skills. Children are ready for a star chart when they reach the age of five or six; a star is marked on a chart to record children's successes, and a reward is earned at the end of the day or at the end of the week. Regardless of which system you're using, the basic rule is to *keep it simple* so that both you and the child know what is expected and what the reward will be.

Stickers for Toddlers

Toddlers love to earn stickers, especially if they are colorful and interesting (dinosaurs, rockets, bugs, and so on). Combining stickers with praise and hugs provides a tangible incentive (something you can see and touch) for children's positive efforts. This makes the reinforcement effect much stronger in terms of strengthening behavior. You can use this combination of stickers and praise to teach a variety of new skills during your child's early years.

Because toilet training is a major milestone during the toddler to preschool years, we'll use it as an example. Let's look in as Mom and Dad use stickers to toilet train their two-year-old daughter, Nadia.

The scene. Mom and Dad had been looking forward to teaching Nadia how to use a toilet. Nadia had followed Mom into the bathroom

Rudy Takes a Liking to His Sticker Chart

Rudy, see this chart? It's for you. If you do a chore by 9:00 A.M. on Saturday, you get a red sticker. And if you cooperate, you get a green sticker, and you get double blue stickers for telling us that you have to go to the bathroom. . . . Rudy, are you following me?

Rudy, don't eat the sticker chart, please. . . . Now, on Tuesdays, you will be on plan A and . . . Rudy, son, please don't eat the sticker chart . . .

on several occasions and asked about going potty, so Mom and Dad bought a new potty chair and placed it prominently in the bathroom. When Nadia showed some interest in the potty chair, they set aside a weekend to help her learn this new skill.

Mom: (walking into the bathroom) Nadia, come in here. I want to talk to you about something. (Nadia scampers into the bathroom. Mom points to the potty chair.) Do you remember what this is?

Nadia: Potty, Mom!

Mom: That's right. This is *your* potty chair! Now that you're a big girl, you're ready to use the potty, just like Mom and Dad. Let's try it without really going potty. (She puts Nadia on the seat.) That's great! (calls to Dad in the other room) Look, Dad, Nadia is trying the new potty chair.

Dad: (with enthusiasm) Good job, Nadia! Can you use the potty?

Nadia: (looking very proud of herself) Yes, I can. (claps her hands)

Mom: That's great! And when you use the your potty chair, I'm going to give you a sticker like this one. (She puts a dinosaur sticker on Nadia's shirt.) Tell us when you need to go potty, and we'll help you try the new potty chair. Okay?

Nadia: (looking excited) Okay!

The first time Nadia used the potty chair, Mom and Dad clapped and cheered—all the noise nearly jolted her off the chair! Every time she used the potty that weekend, Mom or Dad put a colorful sticker on her clothes and praised her achievement. Nadia loved this new "game" of using the potty chair. By the end of the weekend she was a very proud, nearly toilet-trained two-year-old.

Sticker Charts for Three- and Four-Year-Olds

By the time children reach the age of three or four, they are ready to start using a *simple* sticker chart instead of having a sticker put on their hand or on their clothes. Again, it's best to focus on only one skill or bad habit at a time. A sticker chart is visually oriented in that the colorful stickers placed on the chart show the child's progress without requiring any reading skills.

To make it effective, the stickers should be placed on the chart *immediately* after the desired behavior, with lots of praise and fanfare for the child's positive efforts. The Stickersaurus is an example of a sticker chart that would be fun for young children.

Let's look at how a chart like this could be used to teach cooperation to a young child who is having troubling minding her parents' requests. The first step is to create a chart similar to the Stickersaurus (or you can copy one of the blank charts provided at the end of this chapter). It's a good idea to make sure you have plenty of colorful stickers on hand before you get started.

The next step is to introduce the idea of using a sticker chart to your child. For a three-year-old, the explanation would go something like this: "Bonita, we're going to try something new. See these stickers? Every time you mind, you get a sticker. Do you know what minding means? When I ask you to put your toys away and you do it, that's minding. Now let's pretend. Bonita, please put your ball in the basket. (Bonita does so.) That's great! You just earned a sticker for doing such a good job. Let's go put it on the chart over here." That's all the explanation necessary.

If Bonita's parents want to give her an extra reward for cooperating three or more times a day, they can. But at her age, Bonita needs the immediate reward of getting a sticker or putting a sticker on a chart, with praise as

Stickersaurus

an extra incentive. If she gets an extra reward, such as going on a walk with Mom or Dad, the reward should be connected with the chart by saying, "Bonita, look (pointing to the sticker chart), you have three stickers! You really have been minding today! Great! You know what that means? You get to do something special. Do you want to go on a walk or on a bike ride to the park? You choose."

It's important for both parents to give stickers for the behavior they have selected to work on. This gives a consistent message to the child that helps her connect the behavior with receiving the incentive. Again, the reward needs to be given immediately.

Star Charts for Four- and Five-Year-Olds

As children grow older, they are able to work toward goals that span the course of a day or more. When children reach the age of four or five, the visually oriented sticker chart can be replaced with a star chart like the one seen here (blank charts are provided at the end of this chapter). With a star chart, the child earns points during the day (which are recorded as stars drawn on the chart) and receives an incentive in the evening. Once the child is successful with a daily chart, the time span can be gradually increased to several days or perhaps a week.

Star charts require more planning because parents need to be very clear about three important details: (1) what time of day the chart will be discussed; (2) how many points (stars) are required to earn an incentive; and (3) what incentive the child will earn. A plan that includes these three details will make it easier for you to follow through and be consistent.

To make planned incentives work, make sure that every day your child is reminded of his progress in a positive way. It's best to do this at the same time each day. Here's an example of a mother discussing a star chart with her five-year-old daughter, Jennifer. The focus was co-operating with requests, which is an ongoing issue with most children. Mom picked 7 P.M.—just after dinner—to sit down with Jennifer and re-view her progress on the chart for that day. She begins the discussion with "Let's look at your chart. How did you do today?" Sitting down with Jennifer, she points to the stars for that day. "All right, you got four stars today for cooperation! You only needed three for your reward, so it's time for you to pick something fun. What do you want to do: play

Star Chart

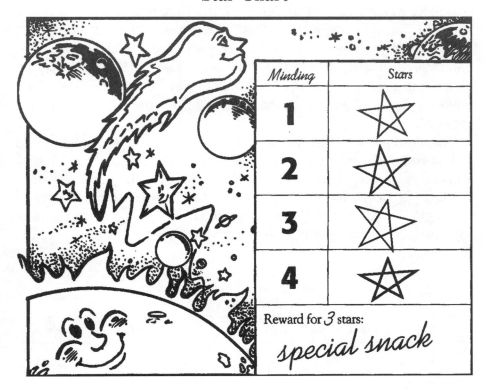

Minding	Stars
1	☆
2	☆
3	☆
4	☆

Reward for *3* stars: *special snack*

hide and seek, read a story with me in bed, or have a special snack?"

For five-year-olds, putting a star on the chart should be a special family event as well. If Jennifer cooperates when Mom asks her to bring her juice container into the kitchen, Mom says, "Thanks for helping. You get another star on your chart for cooperation!" Putting a star on the chart encourages your child's continued positive effort. By providing another reward for stars, your child also learns to put forth a sustained effort to cooperate. This helps the child learn to work toward larger goals, something that becomes increasingly important both at home and at school as children grow older.

When reviewing the child's progress on the chart, it's important to be upbeat and encouraging regardless of whether she earns the reward or not. Again, focus on her positive efforts. If, in the previous example, Jennifer had earned only one star on her chart for that day, Mom could have said, "You cooperated once today, and that's good. You needed two more to get a reward. If you try just a little harder tomorrow, I'm sure you'll be able to get three stars!" Keep your statement short; don't get involved in a lengthy discussion or give a lecture on the virtues of cooperation. Simply set the stage for success on the following day by expressing confidence in the child's ability to earn the reward. If the child repeatedly fails to earn the reward, reduce the number of points required.

Because parents often have problems getting young children to go to bed without a fuss, let's talk about how a star chart could be used to work on this issue. Going to bed involves several steps: putting pajamas on, brushing teeth, and then going to bed when asked (and, of course, staying in bed). Each of these steps would earn a star on the bedtime star chart. Note that the child earns a reward for receiving all three stars on a given day.

Weekly Star Chart

	Put pajamas on	*Brush teeth*	*Go to bed when asked*
Sunday			
Monday			
Tuesday			
Wednesday			
Thursday			
Friday			
Saturday			

Reward for *3* stars: *10 minutes of extra reading time*

If you find that your child earns the incentive less than 80 percent of the time (four out of five days), then you have set your standards too high. The strategy is to build on the child's successes, which means that you have to start with the child's current level of functioning—and every child is different. For cooperation, it's best to keep track of how often you make a request and how often your child cooperates. A planning chart for cooperation has been provided as an example. Once you have an idea of the child's current level of cooperation, set the standard just above that level.

Planning Chart for Cooperation

Instructions: Every time you make a request, circle the next number; show the child's response under the number: + for cooperating, – for not cooperating.

Your requests:	1	2	3	4	5	6	7	8	9	10
Child's response:	–	+	+	–	+	–	–	+	+	+

For example, if you find that you make an average of about six requests in a day and your four-year-old usually cooperates with three of them, you should start off with four as the standard. Then see how it goes. To be effective, a star chart usually needs some fine tuning. As the child's skills improve, you can gradually raise the number of successes needed to earn the reward. Once your child is consistently earning rewards for a fully developed skill or for breaking a bad habit, move on and use the chart to focus on something else (but continue to comment on the child's success with that particular skill).

A star chart can also provide support for a child who is learning to do a simple chore. It should be a task that isn't too complicated, like putting dirty clothes in the clothes hamper, dusting, emptying the trash, feeding the cat, making the bed, or sweeping the front porch. Even at age four, children are challenged by a chore that involves two or three steps. Again, it's very important for the child to be successful, and to receive rewards for his positive efforts and incentives to maintain those efforts. Keep in mind that every child is unique and has different abilities.

Children naturally enjoy becoming more competent and effective in their world. Parents can build on this natural tendency in children by approaching skill development in a positive, upbeat way—for example, "Jennifer, I think you're old enough now to make your bed like your sister." Breaking the task into small steps will make it easier for the child to complete the task successfully. When you begin working on a new chore, reward the child for learning how to do each of the necessary steps. The following bed-making chart was used to help four-year-old Jennifer learn to make her own bed.

Notice that the way star charts are used is very similar to the way weekly allowance systems work with school-age children: The child does chores or tasks during the week and receives an allowance on the weekend for the chores completed. By getting started early with stickers, sticker charts, and star charts, the transition to an allowance system should go smoothly.

Bed-Making Chart

	Pillow in its place	*Straighten sheets*	*Straighten blanket*	*All done*
Sunday				
Monday				
Tuesday				
Wednesday				
Thursday				
Friday				
Saturday				

Reward if bed is made ("all done") for *4* days: *rent a movie*

The Good Behavior Game

A game-like approach can be used to support children's efforts to eliminate bad habits and develop self-control. The game involves giving stickers or other incentives for certain periods of the day that your child showed "good behavior." This is another way to break a task into smaller steps that make it easier for the child to be successful.

Here's an example of how the Good Behavior Game works. Danny was five years old when his mother decided it was time to help him learn not to suck his thumb. Because this behavior occurred throughout the day, she decided to make it easy for Danny to be successful by dividing the day into morning, afternoon, and evening. Since Mom was with Danny all day almost every day, she would be able to track carefully whether he sucked his thumb. She made a chart by putting the days of the week across the top and drawing a picture of a thumb under each day. She introduced the idea to Danny by telling him that he was a big boy now and that it was time for him to stop sucking his thumb. Then she explained the chart—she said that Danny could put a sticker on a thumb if he had kept his thumb out of his mouth during that time of the day.

Because this was important to Danny's mother, she bought a grab bag of inexpensive but interesting little toys and gadgets to give as rewards. At first, Danny got to pick a reward if he simply earned one sticker for not sucking his thumb during any one of the time periods on the chart. After a week, she increased the requirement to two time periods a day, and later to three, before he earned a reward. In three weeks Danny had stopped sucking his thumb, without nagging or criticism. Note that with some children, it may be necessary to start with smaller time intervals or even certain places in the house; for example, no thumb sucking for 15 minutes, or during dinner, or in the living room, and so on. The idea is to make it easy for the child to be successful and then to build on that success.

The Good Behavior Game also can be used to promote positive behavior among brothers and sisters. Let's see how this works. Manfred and Liz were busy parents of a five-year-old daughter and four-year-old identical twin boys. Sometimes things got out of hand in the playroom before dinner or on weekends. Finally, Liz put a timer in the playroom.

She explained to her children that if they could play nicely with only one reminder for 10 minutes, when the timer went off they would all get a sticker. Manfred carefully explained that playing nicely meant "no yelling, calling each other names, grabbing toys, or hitting. Now, what does playing nicely mean?" After they answered, he asked, "And what will you get if you play nicely until the timer goes off?" Manfred continued to prompt the children until they all could repeat the rules back to him.

Manfred and Liz used a sticker chart to keep track of their children's positive play. For the first day, Manfred and Liz only had one Good Behavior Game, a 10-minute session on a Saturday morning. They picked this time for two reasons: first, because it was the easiest for them to monitor, and second, because the kids usually played well—they wanted this first game to be successful. After a couple of successes they moved the Good Behavior Game to just before dinner during weeknights. Eventually they raised the standard so that the children had to earn two stickers before they received a reward. Manfred and Liz only had to use the Good Behavior Game every now and then to control the kids' arguing and fighting during playtime.

The advantages of offering a group reward is that it compels children to cooperate with one another to reduce the arguing and fighting among themselves. Because Manfred and Liz were very consistent about using the plan and following through with the rewards, the children also became more responsive to reminders about playing nicely.

Summary

Children need lots of support and motivation to change their behavior. In the previous chapter we discussed how parents can use positive attention (praise, hugs, and so on) as incentives for their children's good behavior; these incentives are important because they are effective and can be given immediately, and because there is an endless supply of them. The focus of this chapter is on combining positive attention with a structured approach to using tangible incentives. Stickers, sticker charts, and star charts are powerful tools that help children learn new skills, enhance their self-control, and break bad habits.

One of the major issues in supporting a child's positive efforts is being realistic about the child's abilities. As children move through toddlerhood into the preschool and school-age years, their range of abilities changes quickly. Their ability to make the connection between their positive efforts and receiving a rewards and incentives also improves with age. We suggest that you use immediate rewards (placing a colorful sticker on their hand or clothes) for children who are two to three years old. When children reach the age of three or four, a visually oriented sticker chart can be used. A star chart that is tied to a reward can be used when children reach the age of four or five.

The Good Behavior Game was introduced as a positive approach to teaching new skills that involve self-control. The game creates opportunities for children to take small steps in changing a behavior (such as not sucking their thumb during certain periods of the day) and in earning rewards as a group for good behavior (such as playing nicely).

• • • • • • • • • • •

Home Practice Activity

Basic Skill (Time required: 20 minutes)
Decide what positive behavior or new skill you would like to work on, and then select the incentive system you will use to support that behavior: stickers on the child's hand or clothing (toddlers), a sticker chart (three- and four-year-olds), or a star chart (four- and five-year-olds). With two- and three-year-olds, it's best to begin by focusing on one thing: for example, a simple chore (helping to put the toys away) *or* cooperation. A four-year-old can earn stickers for doing a simple chore *and* for cooperation. Reread the parts of this chapter that apply to your situation and then prepare the necessary materials: stickers, charts, and/or backup incentives (small prizes); blank charts that you may photocopy are provided at the end of this chapter.

Pick a day to work on the positive behavior you have selected—it should be a day when you will be spending some relatively unstructured time with your child (for example, dinner time or Saturday morning). Introduce the idea of using stickers/stars charts to your child. Tell your child exactly what he needs to do to earn the stickers/stars and what the prize is (offering a reward is optional).

Post the chart on the refrigerator or some other place that is easy to see. Young children may enjoy coloring the chart before you put it into use; this will help them feel included in the activity and attract their attention to the chart.

Remember to keep your plan simple and your goals modest. Consider your child's skill level and begin from there. If she doesn't earn a sticker right away, your goals are probably too high (she should be successful about 80 percent of the time). It's important for her to be successful, or she will stop trying. Now it's time for you to get started!

Optional: Practice using the Good Behavior Game.

Advanced Skill (Time required: 60 minutes)
Now we want you to fine-tune your approach. For this practice you will continue using the stickers/stars charts that you set up in the basic skill activity, but we want you to take a careful look at your child's success rate. If your child is earning the stickers/stars most of the time (at least four times out of five) and seems to be making good progress, keep it up! If your child is not responding well to the incentive system, here is a list of troubleshooting tips to try.

Problem	Possible Solution
• Child tries but doesn't earn a reward	• Reduce your requirements for giving a reward
• Child doesn't do a good job (e.g., cleaning room)	• Break the chore or skill into smaller steps
• Child is unmotivated	• Check to see how often child gets other rewards without having to work
	• Catch the child being good and give a reward, at least two to three times a day
	• Change rewards

Above all, don't get discouraged—it often takes a little time and some fine tuning to make incentive systems work.

Stickersaurus

*Suggestion: Enlarge on a photocopier to create additional charts;
have your child participate by asking him or her to color the background.*

Star Chart

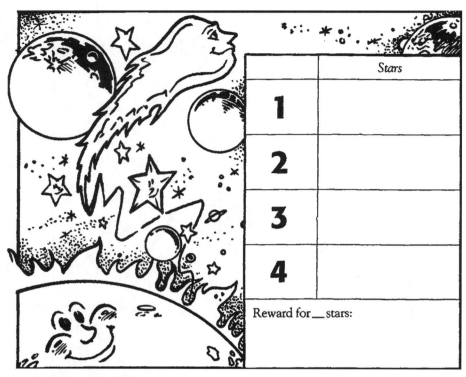

	Stars
1	
2	
3	
4	
Reward for __ stars:	

Suggestion: Enlarge on a photocopier to create additional charts;
have your child participate by asking him or her to color the background.

Weekly Star Chart for _____

Sunday			
Monday			
Tuesday			
Wednesday			
Thursday			
Friday			
Saturday			

Reward:

CHAPTER FIVE

....

Setting Limits on Misbehavior

The scene. Dad has volunteered to take his five-year-old son, River, and two other boys to the park. When they reach the park, the boys immediately run over to a large play structure shaped like a ship, surrounded by sand and dirt, and begin to play "Pirates of the Caribbean." Soon, however, the game gets carried away and the boys begin throwing sand at each other.

Dad: (looking somewhat concerned, but sounding timid) Boys, I don't like what I'm seeing over there. How do you think it feels to have sand thrown in your face?

River: (shrugging his shoulders) It's okay, Dad—we're just playing. (His friends run wildly around the play structure as River bends down to grab another handful of sand.)

Clearly, it's time for Dad to set limits on the boys' play. If Dad doesn't do something soon, tempers may flare or someone will get hurt. So much for having an afternoon of fun at the park! How would you feel if your child were playing with these boys? Most parents would be justifiably peeved because Dad isn't doing his job, which is to supervise the boys while they are at the park and to set limits if necessary.

Children need both encouragement and limits. As we saw in Chapters Three and Four, encouragement provides an incentive for children to develop new skills and break bad habits. Setting limits defines the boundaries for acceptable behavior. It's a lot like driving a car: Encouragement provides the fuel that makes the car go, and limits define the edge of the road. If the car isn't given guidance, it's likely to stall or swerve off the road!

Children Need Clear Limits

All children misbehave or push the rules every now and then. It takes time for them to learn the boundaries for acceptable behavior, particularly if the boundaries are not clear. As we have mentioned in previous chapters, *consistency is the key to successful parenting,* and the same is true for setting limits. When children misbehave, it's up to parents, teachers, and other adults to set reasonable and consistent limits on their behavior.

There are two sides of the coin for effective limit setting: clearly stating the rules and providing consequences when the rules are broken. These two aspects of limit setting go hand-in-hand. Your child needs to learn where you have set the boundaries on her behavior. This means you have to be clear in your own mind about what you think is acceptable and what is not—regardless of your mood or how tired you may be. And when the rules are broken, you have to follow through with mild consequences that are effective and over quickly. Children learn best by experiencing consequences; talking, lecturing, or nagging about rules simply doesn't work.

Typically, most parents begin setting limits when toddlers are old enough to explore the world around them and safety issues become a real concern. Toddlers and young children must learn not to touch the stove, not to go near the stairs, not to pull the dog's ears, not to throw their toys, and so on. Children must discover many of life's lessons for themselves, through hundreds of trial-and-error experiences that should be carefully guided and supervised by a caring adult. This is not always easy, however, as we see in the following example.

The scene. Four-year-old Tashia is two steps ahead of Mom as they approach the crosswalk. Mom yells, "Wait for me—I need to hold your hand when we cross the street," but Tashia doesn't listen. As Tashia steps off the curb, Mom manages to grab her hand in the nick of time, for just then a car turns the corner and passes in front of them. Mom is unnerved by the incident, and while they cross the street together, she reminds Tashia of the rule about always waiting at the crosswalk and holding Mom's hand when crossing a street.

Most of us have found ourselves in situations like this. In spite of our best efforts to ensure the safety of our children, they always seem to find a way to scare the living daylights out of us. Although Tashia probably learned something from this experience, it was a close call. It would be much better if Tashia learns to obey the rule about crossing the street. The question is, what's the best way to teach young children *not* to do something? First, children must learn to cooperate with rules and requests from adults (discussed in Chapters One and Two). Second, parents have to set clear limits on their children's behavior.

Four Steps for Setting Limits

There are four simple steps for effective limit setting: (1) Get the child's attention, (2) Clearly state the rule, (3) Tell the child what to do instead of misbehaving, and (4) Give the child a warning or a consequence. Let's consider these steps one at a time.

1. Get the child's attention. Young children's minds are often lost in their immediate activity, and they are highly distractible. A basic skill when spending time with young children is getting their attention and then talking to them in terms they understand (not baby talk). This skill also applies to limit setting: *Make sure the child is listening when you state the rule.* Making eye contact with the child is important; it may be helpful to kneel down so you're looking directly at the child. This makes it easier for the child to tune you in and tune out distractions. It's up to you to get the child's attention constructively. Sometimes this means getting a response before you go any further; you might say, "Tashia, please look at me when I'm talking to you."

2. Clearly state the rule. The father who took the boys to the park could have said, "Okay, boys, no more sand throwing" in a neutral but firm tone of voice. Don't bring up problems from the past or give a lecture. You can explain why the rule is necessary some other time. *A child's misbehavior is rarely due to a lack of understanding about the* *rules.* Focus instead on interrupting the child's misbehavior. A short statement that tells the child what she is doing wrong will produce the best results. For example, don't say, "Stop chasing the dog around the house. You are going to hurt yourself or break something. You know I have told you not to do that a million times. Now STOP IT!!" Parents tend to use statements like this (we call it "nattering") when they're frustrated, tired, or angry, but *this approach to limit setting does not change the child's behavior.* An approach that is more likely to get co-operation without creating any new problems is to say something like "No running in the house—if you want to run, take the dog outside."

3. Tell the child what to do. This brings us to *redirecting,* which is probably the most useful skill for parents of young children. When you tell children what *not to do,* it's important to tell them what they *can do* instead. This may sound simple, but it takes practice. Here are some examples: "No candy before lunch—would you like some sliced apples?" After stating the rule about no sand throwing, the father who took the boys to the park could have redirected their attention to another activity (which would prevent further sand throwing) by saying, "Check out that rocket ship. Let's see who can climb to the top first."

Skilled preschool teachers are experts at redirecting children's attention. They rarely get to step four because they are good at watching, anticipating problems, and redirecting children to new activities or positive behaviors. The most challenging type of redirecting is one that teaches the child a new skill. For example, in an upbeat tone of voice you might say, "Tashia, when you get to the street, I want you to stop, turn around, and wait for me. Take my hand and we will cross the street together!"

4. Give the child a warning or a consequence. All children need consequences every now and then to help them learn not to misbehave. *Many parents overuse warnings and underuse consequences.* Perhaps this is because they don't have the tools they need to give effective and sane consequences. We recommend giving no more than one warning before using a consequence—for example, "Okay, you guys, no sand throwing—the next time I see one of you throwing sand, that will be a time out." (Time out is explained in detail in the next chapter.) Here's a slightly different example: "If you're still chasing the dog by the time I count to three, it will be a time out."

There are two important parts in these statements. First, the warning is presented as an "if/then" statement. This makes it clear to the child what he must do to avoid the consequence. Notice that in the second example, the parent counts to three; sometimes it helps to count because it gives the child a chance to cooperate: Cooperation requires "shifting gears." If the child continues to misbehave after the warning, it's time to give him a gentle consequence.

Shifting Gears to Appropriate Behavior

If we think of misbehavior as going backward, then positive behavior is moving forward. The way you respond to children's problem behaviors plays an important role in helping them shift gears to appropriate behavior. There are several ways to help your child shift out of reverse gear: providing a distraction, ignoring misbehavior, allowing natural consequences, and choosing corrective consequences. Let's take a look at how these strategies are used.

Using Distractions

As we mentioned earlier, toddlers and young children are easily distracted. When young children misbehave, you can often help them make the transition to appropriate behavior by offering a distraction. For example, if your child is pestering you for another cookie, you could say, "No, you can't have another cookie right now, but I want to show you something. Look at the kitty sitting in the sun on the couch over there. Doesn't she look warm and snuggly?" Another option, discussed earlier, is to redirect the child to a positive alternative, such as having an apple instead of a cookie. Distraction and redirection work well with toddlers and very young children. As children grow older, however, this strategy becomes less effective.

Ignoring Misbehavior

At times it may be best to simply ignore the child. For example, young children may become angry when they don't get their way, and they may say hurtful things such as "I hate you." In this situation you should ignore the child rather than try to talk him out of feeling that way. Talking to the child about the hurtful words just makes the problem worse because it gives the child attention for misbehaving. At times like these, children need some time to calm down.

Allowing Natural Consequences

Using natural consequences involves letting the child directly experience the consequences of her behavior. For example, if your child refuses to put gloves on when it's cold outside, put the gloves in your pocket and let her find out why it's important to wear gloves in cold weather. When her hands get cold, just give her the gloves—don't lecture. Obviously, this approach should be used only when the natural consequences won't hurt the child.

Choosing Corrective Consequences

Corrective consequences simply prompt the positive behavior that you would prefer in place of the problem behavior. For example, to use a corrective consequence when you see your toddler grabbing a toy from her sister, you might say, "Maria, no grabbing. If you want a toy, say please. Now say, 'Toy, please.'" If Maria follows the prompt, reward her cooperation by saying, "Very good," and by giving her the toy.

With young children, *many teaching opportunities are best handled with neutral or even positive responses* such as the one illustrated in the example involving Maria. Redirecting, which was discussed earlier, also emphasizes teaching a positive behavior. Both of these techniques work well with toddlers and young children who need help with shifting gears to appropriate alternatives. When using either corrective consequences or redirecting, remember to reward positive behavior with attention, praise, hugs, and other incentives. This helps turn limit setting into a positive learning experience and avoids power struggles.

A Note about Consequences

Parents often hesitate to use consequences that are not unpleasant for the child. The idea seems to be that the child will not learn unless the consequence is painful. This belief has led many parents to use physical punishments such as spanking and slapping the child's hand. We do not recommend using physical punishment with children for the following reasons: (1) Adults tend to use this consequence when they are angry, which means it is used inconsistently; (2) It frightens and humiliates the child; (3) It may set up patterns that lead to abusive behavior; and (4) Other consequences that don't have these drawbacks are actually more effective in changing the child's behavior.

The Importance of Consistent Limits

Setting limits really brings out differences in parenting styles, often going back to the way parents were raised themselves (an idea explored in the home practice activity in the Introduction). Some parents think it's harmful to discipline children or to set limits on their behavior. "Permissive" parents feel that children's need for independence and freedom of expression is more important than following adult-imposed rules. "Authoritarian" parents, on the other hand, believe that children need close supervision and firm guidance from adults. As it turns out, neither of these extremes in parenting styles is healthy. Children who are raised without limits often develop severe behavior problems; they spend far more time whining, teasing, hitting, and having tantrums than other children their age. As adults, these children find it difficult to deal with the realities of work and social living, where limits are imposed by others. Children with authoritarian parents, on the other hand, are usually relatively well behaved but tend to be withdrawn, anxious, or unsure of themselves.

Parents often have strong feelings about what they consider to be misbehavior. Some parents will tolerate whining but won't accept messiness. Others will tolerate tantrums but won't accept rudeness. Most adults, however, would agree that hitting is not acceptable. When your child goes to daycare or preschool, other adults become involved in setting boundaries on your child's behavior. Whether you are dealing with misbehavior at home or reports from daycare about your child's exploits, it's important to know what kind of behavior you are willing to accept in your child and to set limits on behaviors you feel are inappropriate.

Children must receive consistent messages about limits. *If children receive mixed messages about limits, they will test the limits more often.* In an ideal situation, the limits on a child's behavior would be the same whether she is at home, in daycare, staying with her grandparents, or spending time with a babysitter. Although it's almost impossible to create an ideal environment for your child, you can work toward this goal by discussing your approach to limit setting with your partner. Remember that people are more receptive if you use phrases like "I would prefer that . . . " instead of *demanding* that they adopt your approach. Try to respect the fact that other people may have different feelings about setting limits.

Summary

Setting limits is an important part of your job as a parent. It's just as important as providing love and encouragement. When you are setting limits, focus on the immediate goal: to prevent or interrupt your child's misbehavior without getting angry. Try to view the situation as an opportunity to teach your child to replace misbehavior with appropriate alternatives. Above all, you need to be consistent to help your child learn the boundaries you have set for acceptable behavior.

Although limit setting can be difficult, your skills will improve with practice. Knowing the best way to respond to children's problem behavior takes experience and a bit of intuition. As you are working on your skills, make sure you review the four steps for limit setting outlined in this chapter. These steps, which are the keys to success, are as follows: get your child's attention, clearly state the rule, redirect or prompt positive behavior, and (if all else fails) use a consequence.

We discussed several ways to help children shift gears when they are misbehaving: providing distractions, ignoring misbehavior, allowing natural consequences, and choosing corrective consequences. These are gentle ways to interrupt and discourage misbehavior. In Chapter Six we will discuss another very useful consequence: time out. When parents use these methods consistently, children quickly learn what is expected of them, and family life becomes more peaceful and enjoyable for everyone.

• • • • • • • • • • •

Home Practice Activity

Basic Skill (Time required: 10 minutes)

If you are part of a two-parent family, begin by discussing your approach to limit setting with your partner. Review the list of typical problem behaviors below and talk about the kinds of behaviors you are concerned about and what you think should be done to prevent them. You don't have to agree; simply discussing your approach is a good start.

One of the keys to effective limit setting is knowing how to state the rule clearly when misbehavior occurs. Now circle one or two of the problem behaviors that you would like to work on. If you are a two-parent family, do this together. Don't attempt to change more than one or two behaviors at a time—you can work on the others later. For your first attempts at limit setting, pick something that you see fairly often; for the reasons described in Chapter Two, not minding is an excellent choice. After you have made your selection, practice with your partner stating the rule for each misbehavior (it may be helpful to review the section presented earlier in this chapter titled "Step 2: Clearly State the Rule"). Remember to keep the rule short and to the point. If you feel confident enough, try stating the rule when your child misbehaves.

Typical Problem Behaviors

Not minding	Whining
Hitting	Teasing
Temper tantrums	Rough-handling pets
Throwing or intentionally breaking toys	Messiness, not putting toys away
Not staying in bed all night	Thumb sucking
Name-calling, saying mean things to others	Baby talk
Wetting pants	Yelling
Crying	Spitting
Not sharing	Rudeness, poor manners
Swearing	

Advanced Skill (Time required: 50 minutes)
Pick up to three of the problem behaviors from the list provided in the Basic Skill section, practice stating the rule for each one, and decide which of the following consequences you will use when you see the behavior: distraction, ignoring, natural consequences, or corrective consequences. Use the form provided to write down the details of your plan. If you have time, role-play with your partner (or a friend, if you are a single parent) how you will respond when you see the problem behavior; for example, state the rule and redirect the child to a positive behavior.

Limit-Setting Plan

Misbehavior _____

State the rule _____

_____

Consequence for misbehavior _____

_____

_____

Limit-Setting Plan

Misbehavior _____

State the rule _____

_____

Consequence for misbehavior _____

_____

_____

Limit-Setting Plan

Misbehavior _____

State the rule _____

_____

Consequence for misbehavior _____

_____

_____

If you feel comfortable using the plan you have just created to work on your child's misbehavior, give it a try! Don't worry if your plan doesn't produce results right away. In the next chapter, we'll discuss some additional consequences that you can use to correct misbehavior.

Optional: Watch how parents with young children do or don't set limits when they are in public places. When you are in a restaurant or grocery store, pay attention to the children's behavior and their parents' responses. Then think about whether you want your child to behave like the children you are watching. What happens when parents are too strict with their children? What happens when they're too permissive?

CHAPTER SIX

•••

Using Consequences and Time Out

The scene. Five-year-old Kenshi is playing on the living room floor with his three-year-old sister, Yokiko. Dad is making lunch in the kitchen when suddenly he hears a commotion in the living room.

Dad: (seeing Yokiko sitting on the floor, crying) What's going on here? Yokiko, what's the matter?

Yokiko: (sobbing) Kenshi hit me because I wouldn't give him the truck.

Kenshi: (jumping up, with the truck in his hands) It's mine! She wouldn't give it to me.

Dad: (firmly, in a neutral tone of voice) You know the rule, Kenshi: No hitting. That's a time out. (Dad takes Kenshi by the hand and leads him out of the room.)

Young children often have problems when it comes to sharing toys at playtime. In this scene, Dad was very matter-of-fact in his approach. It didn't take long for him to take stock of the situation and determine that Kenshi had broken a well-established house rule: No hitting. Then, without lecturing, he gave Kenshi a time out as a consequence. This approach will help Kenshi learn not to hit his sister, or other children either.

This scene illustrates two important points about using a consequence: It should be used immediately, and without lectures or anger. Before we discuss how to use time out as a consequence, let's take a look at some general guidelines for using consequences with young children.

Keeping Consequences SANE

We have developed what we call SANE guidelines for using consequences that are based on more than 20 years of work with families. These guidelines ensure that the consequences you use with children are both effective and constructive in promoting children's positive behavior. A good consequence is Small, Avoids punishing the parent, is Nonabusive to the child, and is Effective. Let's review each of the SANE guidelines.

1. Small Consequences Are Better

It's better to give a consequence that is too small than one that is too serious. Research has shown that *children learn more* (that is, their behavior changes more) *from small consequences*. It's tempting to give a child a big consequence when you're angry, but it's unlikely that you will follow through later when you have calmed down. Also, young children may need several consequences on some days, and a mild consequence such as a time out can be used throughout the day, if necessary.

2. Avoid Punishing Yourself

This may seem like an odd statement, but consider the child who acts out in a shopping mall or restaurant; wouldn't it be better to *prevent* this situation by using an effective consequence that teaches the child to cooperate while you're shopping? In moments of exhaustion, parents often select consequences that are more punishing to themselves than to the child, such as dragging a crying child out of the store and driving home or simply not going to public places because of their child's behavior. Sitting at the side of your child's bed for hours every night as a consequence for her crying or calling out is clearly punishing for you and disruptive to your marriage!

3. Never Abuse Your Child

Parents rarely hurt their children intentionally. Verbal and physical abuse are destructive to the child and to you as well. As we mentioned in Chapter Five, we do not recommend using physical punishments.

Although some parents may have experienced this type of discipline as a child, now is the time to break the cycle! With some conscious effort (and perhaps some help from a good therapist), it is possible!

The best way to prevent abusive discipline is to avoid giving consequences when you are upset. Several methods for managing your negative emotions were discussed in the Introduction. Remember that the goal is to not to punish the child, but to *teach* the child not to misbehave and to encourage appropriate behavior in its place. A good teacher is patient and understanding.

4. Effective Consequences Are Consistent Consequences

Use consequences that are under your control, that can be used immediately, and that remove the reinforcement for the child's misbehavior. The mild consequences and four steps for effective consequences outlined in Chapter Five work well in most situations. The time out procedure, which is described next, is also very effective.

One of the most overlooked aspects of working with children is that they are amazingly sensitive learners. Gentle consequences that are consistently applied are all that is needed to change behavior. Contrary to popular beliefs, it isn't necessary to use severe consequences to "make an impression on the child." An added benefit is that *it actually takes less work to use the SANE approach to setting limits,* and it allows you to maintain an upbeat and positive atmosphere in your family.

Using Time Out

After considering the SANE guidelines, it's easy to see why a time out is the consequence of choice for young children. It's effective, easy to use, nonabusive, and nonpunishing to the parent (that is, it's over quickly). The basic approach is to interrupt children's misbehavior by removing them from the social situation and placing them in a boring place where they can't disrupt others. For very young children, you can put a chair in a hallway or a corner of the room—somewhere that children will not be able to receive attention from others. It's best to put older children in a separate room such as the bathroom (*not* in their bedroom with all their toys). If a separate room is used, all of the dangerous or messy items must be removed first.

Time out should be very brief; a one-minute time out effectively interrupts the child's misbehavior, so this is where you start. If the child refuses to go to time out, add one minute for each reminder; for example, "Okay, that's two minutes . . . (child still doesn't go to time out) That's three minutes . . . " and so on. This continues until you reach a total of five minutes of time out. If the child still refuses to go, a privilege is removed as a backup consequence for not cooperating; for example, "Since you are not going to time out like I asked you to, Susan will have to go home now." You get the idea.

You can begin using time out with children who are two years old, but five minutes is a long time to expect them to stay in one place. Try to keep it short. Long time outs can create more problems than they solve. Remember: You want to build on success. Having your child go to time out for the specified amount of time empowers you to be effective in setting limits for your child.* Score a point for the parent!

Here's how it works. If you have a two-parent family, discuss the idea of using time out with your spouse or partner. Time out will be effective only if both parents use it in the same way. If you have worked through the home practice activity in Chapter Five, you have already selected a problem behavior to work on. Remember that it should be something you see several times a day that you both agree is a problem. Not minding, hitting, swearing, and throwing toys are good choices.

Telling Your Children about Time Out

The next step is to introduce the idea of using time out to your children. Tell them that you are going to start sending them to time out when you see them breaking certain rules (describe the problem behavior you have selected). *Emphasize that this new approach will make it more peaceful around the house because you won't have to get angry or nag them about their behavior.* Tell them that after they go to time out, they can continue playing.

It's important to review the details of the time out procedure with young children, keeping the discussion light and even humorous. Then you should

---

Scot's note: In our family we used time out with Gus, the dog, too. It worked great, but it was a bit confusing for him sometimes. When we would tell our son, Kobin, "All right, that's a time out," Gus would hang his head and walk into the bathroom.

role-play a time out with your child. Tell your child that you want to show him how time out works. Put a chair in the corner and tell him you're going to pretend he just hit the dog. State the rule and the consequence: "No hitting the dog. That's a time out." Take your child by the hand to the time-out chair in the hallway or bathroom and say how long time out will last as you set the timer. Tell him there will be no arguing or talking while he is in time out. When the timer bell rings, say, "Okay, your time out is over—that's all there is to it! If you go to time out right away, it will only last one minute. Each time I have to remind you, I'll have to add another minute."

It's also a good idea for you and your child to practice adding extra minutes for the child's refusal to go to time out. Role-playing this helps her experience the difference between cooperating and not cooperating with time out. You might say, "Okay, this time I want you to ignore me every time I ask you to go to time out. Can you do that? Remember that this is pretend, so you're not in trouble. No hitting the dog—please go to time out." (Child pretends to ignore the request.) "That's two minutes." (Child ignores request.) "That's three minutes." This continues until you reach five minutes; then say something like "Okay, you're not cooperating with time out, so no cartoons this morning." End of discussion—no lectures, deals, negotiating, or belittling. Be sure to give the child supportive attention (praise) for participating in this role-playing session with you. Children's cooperation should always be reinforced.

After you have practiced using time out with your child, tell her again which misbehaviors will result in a time out. Keep it simple (particularly with a very young child); don't try to explain *why* you want her to stop doing these things. If you must provide an explanation, make it brief.

Once the consequence is over, look for opportunities to encourage and redirect your child. Let it be a time out for you as well. Try not to hold grudges after time out is finished. When your child approaches you after time out, engage her in a positive activity or conversation that is unrelated to the misbehavior.

Preparing the Time-Out Place

With young children, the place you choose for the time-out chair should be separate from family activity areas (kitchen, living room, and so on). This prevents them from getting attention from others for continued misbehavior. The time-out place should be boring but not frightening (not behind closed doors, not in the basement, and so on). Many families use the hallway, a corner of the room (with furniture separating the time-out place from the rest of the room), or the bathroom with the door open.

Before using the time-out place, make sure it is safe. Remove items that would be dangerous to the child or that could be used to make a mess: toilet paper, cleaning supplies, shaving supplies, and so forth. We recommend that you use a timer because it eliminates questions about how much longer until the time out is over. If the child makes a mess while in time out, have her clean it up before she leaves.

With older children (ages four and up) you may want to close the door to the bathroom during time out because older children can be very persistent about trying to engage you in a discussion or argument while in time out.

Troubleshooting Tips

Your child may try to sabotage time out in several ways. Refusing to go to time out is fairly common. We described how to handle this problem earlier in this chapter: Add extra minutes to the duration of time out one minute at a time, and when you reach a total of five minutes, remove a privilege. In a last-ditch effort to avoid time out, a child may promise to stop doing the misbehavior and insist that time out isn't necessary. When this happens, acknowledge that you hope this will be the case but that he will still have to go to time out for breaking a rule. Sometimes a child will have a full-blown temper tantrum when he is told to go to time out. In this situation, it's best to ignore him until he calms down and then take him to time out. A child may tell you that you are being mean or that he hates you when you tell him to go to time out. Avoid getting involved in any discussion about why time out is necessary; if you must say something, simply respond, "You know the rule is no hitting the dog." It's best to ignore negative comments directed at you—and it may help to reframe these comments by reminding yourself that your child is venting his frustration at the situation (having his behavior corrected) on you, and that you are simply trying to teach him to stop misbehaving (which is part of your role as parent). In general, when children try to sabotage time out, they are just testing whether you really intend to follow through. Once your child discovers that you *do* intend to follow through *every time,* he will gradually become more cooperative with time out to get it over with quickly.

Time Out for Teddy

Another useful variation on the use of time out is to put toys that are being used inappropriately "in time out." For example, if your little girl continues to throw her dolls after you have told her not to, take them away and put them where she can't get them. As you are doing this, tell her, "I told you not to throw your dolls. Now I'm going to put them in time out for five minutes." Set a timer for five minutes and give them back when the time is up. This will help teach her to play nicely with her toys.

Playtime Intermission

I hope these toys get out of time out soon. . . .

Sometimes favorite toys such as "Teddy" can be put into time out for very brief periods to correct problem behavior. Bedtime is a good example. Understandably, young children often do not want to go to bed, and they may call out to their parents for hours if limits are not set. Although it is important to spend some quiet time (at least 10 minutes) when putting children to bed to help them make the transition, you also need to set limits on their calling you back. For example, you might say, "Josh, it's time for bed. You need to stay in your bed quietly, or I'll have to put Teddy in time out." If he continues to call out, and you're sure that all his immediate needs have been met, you can say, "Okay, I'm taking Teddy to time out, but I'll bring him back after you show me that you can lie down quietly for five minutes."

Notes about Limit Setting

First, limit setting is appropriate only when you are sure that your child's basic needs have been met; if your child calls out because he has to go to the bathroom, he is cold, or he is thirsty, it is necessary to attend to these obvious needs. Other needs may be less obvious, such as the need to be comforted after a trying day or because he is scared. Children need to know they are loved and well cared for. To keep this from becoming a stalling tactic, ask your child if there is anything else he needs to do before going to bed. After comforting your child, tell him you'll come back to check on him if is lying quietly in bed. (Offer to leave the door open a bit or to put some soothing music on for him.)

The second thing to keep in mind is that when you start setting limits and using consequences, your child's behavior may actually *get worse* for the first couple of days (particularly if she is used to getting her way). This is a sign that your child isn't used to having limits set on her behavior and that you should stay firm in your efforts. Basically, she is testing your resolve to follow through. If she has been allowed to have frequent tantrums or throw food, it's quite a shock when you start setting limits. She has learned to misbehave through many small steps, and now you must teach her to stop misbehaving by taking small steps in the opposite direction. For this reason, it's very important for you to use time out consistently, even when it's awkward, such as when you're in a public place.

Setting Limits in Public Places

Handling children's problem behavior in a public place, such as a restaurant or grocery store, can be frustrating and humiliating. One reason that children tend to misbehave in public places is that they sense it is a setting where their parents' hands are tied. Not so!

The SANE guidelines give you the tools to help you and your child enjoy the finer sides of public life. If your child has developed some bad habits, it may take some extra work for a week or two before you can really begin to enjoy stepping out with your child.

Here's how it works. Take your child to a grocery store, but don't plan on actually buying groceries. When the child begins to whine for a candy bar or a toy, give him a warning: "No, I'm not going to buy that now. And if you don't stop whining by the time I count to three, I'm going to have to take you outside for a time out." Then slowly count to three. If he doesn't stop whining, take him outside for a time out. If you drove to the store, have him sit in the car while you stand outside for one minute. If you don't have a car, find a safe place where he can sit while you stand about 10 feet away; avoid making eye contact, interacting, or talking to him while he is in the time-out place. When the time out is over, simply say in a neutral tone of voice, "Let's try that again—remember, no whining." Then take the child back into the store. Repeat this until he learns not to whine or until you are worn out.

Taking these "dry run" shopping trips will help you concentrate on teaching your child to behave himself while you are shopping. The same idea holds for taking your child to a restaurant. Remember, though, that some children have more patience and self-control than others, and your expectations may need to be adjusted accordingly. Most young children will have trouble in any situation that demands good behavior for extended periods of time. It's unrealistic to expect some children to wait patiently for 15 minutes to have dinner in a restaurant. Take them to a place where there are things to watch and do, or perhaps bring some paper and crayons to help them make it through this trying situation.

It takes work to help children learn to be well behaved, but it will save time and effort in the long run, and it will also improve your relationship with them. It's much easier to get along with children who are well behaved and well adjusted.

Summary

The SANE guidelines were presented to help you test whether a consequence is constructive or something to be avoided. A good consequence is Small, Avoids punishing the parent, is Nonabusive to the child, and is Effective. The time-out procedure was discussed in detail because it satisfies the SANE guidelines, and it can be used at home and in public places. It's clearly the consequence of choice for young children.

Following the suggestions for limit setting outlined in Chapter Five and this chapter, in combination with the skills for using incentives discussed earlier, will give you the basic tools you need to effectively guide the adjustment of your child. Developing a clear limit-setting plan will help you be more consistent, sensible, and balanced in reacting to your child's problem behavior and in teaching positive alternatives. Clearly, this is very important work. Remember to reward *yourself* for your progress and to support your spouse or partner in his or her attempts to follow through with limit setting and consequences.

· · · · · · · · · · ·

Home Practice Activity

Basic Skill (Time required: 15 minutes)
If you haven't finished the home practice activities in Chapter Five, it would be best to go back and complete them now. Before you can begin to use time out, you must come to an agreement with your partner about the one or two behaviors you will focus on at first. (Other behaviors can be added later.)

Talk with your partner about using time out. Pick a time when you won't be interrupted so you can work out any issues that may come up. Remember that people often have strong feelings about setting limits and using consequences with children; try to respect the other person's opinion and negotiate some middle ground that you can both agree on. If your approach doesn't seem to be working after two or three weeks, read this chapter again and do some fine tuning.

Review the steps for time out together, and try role-playing a typical situation that might come up in your household. (One person plays the part of the parent, the other plays the part of the child.) This can be fun, once you get the hang of it! Again, remember to be supportive of one another—this is difficult work. It's also an area in which many parents tend to be inconsistent, and inconsistency can create many problems later on.

Advanced Skill (Time required: 60 minutes)
Introduce the idea of time out to your child (or children) as described earlier in this chapter and go through at least one "dry run." Now you're ready to give it a try. Remember: Once you begin using time out, make sure you use it *every time* you see the misbehavior you are currently working on.

Finally, we have included a Time-Out Worksheet to help you use the technique effectively. Take a minute to review this worksheet to see if it might be something you can use in your family.

Time-Out Worksheet

1. Describe the problem behavior you will be working on, and state the rule: _____

_____

Will you give a warning first?   Yes ❑ No ❑

How often do you usually see the behavior? (*circle one*)

       sometimes   often
(three or four times a day)   (five or more times a day)

What happened when you tried using time out for this behavior? _____

_____

_____

_____

What strategy worked best? Describe any feelings connected with using time out. How did you handle these feelings? Did your partner support your efforts? _____

_____

_____

_____

_____

_____

2. *(Optional)* Describe a second problem behavior you will be working on, and state the rule: _____

_____

Will you give a warning first?   Yes ❑ No ❑

How often do you usually see the behavior? *(circle one)*

| sometimes | often |
| (three or four times a day) | (five or more times a day) |

What happened when you tried using time out for this behavior? ____

_____

_____

What strategy worked best? Describe any feelings connected with using time out. How did you handle these feelings? Did your partner support your efforts? _____

_____

_____

_____

_____

_____

CHAPTER SEVEN

Coaching Children's Friendships

The scene. It's the first warm day of spring, and Dad is out for a walk with his four-year-old daughter, Briana. As they turn the corner at the end of the street, they see Emily and Jesse playing on tricycles in a nearby driveway. Briana, Emily, and Jesse were play companions last summer. As Dad and Briana approach the driveway, Emily and Jesse have stopped playing and are talking about something—their backs are turned and they don't notice Briana. Briana looks down at the ground and starts to walk past them. Dad sizes up the situation and whispers cheerfully, "Briana, you should say hi when you see your friends." Briana does this, and the two children turn their heads, excitedly yell "Briana!" and come running over to talk to her.

With some gentle prompting from Dad, Briana was readily accepted by her play companions instead of being rejected. As this scene shows, young children often need adult guidance to help them successfully navigate the complex world of peers. The support you give your child as she develops friendship skills gives her a key that will open many doors throughout her lifetime. The toddler and preschool years are perhaps the most important time to encourage your child's growth in basic social skills. At this age, your child's playmates are adaptable and readily form new friendships. Later, as her peers become more critical and exclusive, it will be more difficult for her to develop new friends unless she has good social skills.

Three Essential Social Skills

Children need to develop three types of skills to be accepted by their peers: initiating, sharing and cooperation, and conflict resolution. Let's consider these skills one at a time.

Initiating

The ability to initiate activities and friendships is a very important life skill. If your child doesn't learn to initiate activities and friendships, he will have to wait for things to happen in his life. To take charge of his social world, your child will sometimes need to be the one who starts up activities with friends. In his toddler and preschool years, you will be responsible for arranging many of his play contacts. By the age of five or six he will be ready to practice making some of these arrangements on his own. If your child has difficulties in this area, it may be due to shyness or lack of "tact." To overcome his shyness, your child simply needs your support as he takes *small steps* in developing the skills and confidence he needs to play an active role in shaping his social world.

Other children are not shy; they simply don't know what to say or do when entering a group or inviting someone to play. Although they just want to have a friend, they end up being rejected. If this is the situation with your child, she needs to be taught the skills that will lead to success and acceptance. Again, it's important for you to begin teaching these skills during the preschool years—the reputation your child earns early in life may be hard to change later on.

Sharing and Cooperation

The skills of sharing and cooperation don't come naturally to children because the payoffs aren't obvious right away. After all, a child may not at first understand why she should share a toy that she wants to play with. Over time, with your guidance, she will learn that sharing and cooperation are important skills that build friendships and make play activities more enjoyable for everyone.

As children grow older, they gradually learn the value of making these long-term social investments.

It all begins with turn taking. A good time to help your child learn about turn taking is during parent-child play (discussed in more detail in Chapter Eight). Remember to teach by example (model the behavior) and to support your child's positive efforts. Children are receptive to these learning experiences at a very early age. When two-year-olds come to play, it's important to emphasize that they practice taking turns with toys.

Conflict Resolution

Starting a friendship is one thing; *keeping* a friend is another. The key skill your child needs to keep a friend is knowing how to resolve conflict. Your child will find this skill to be important throughout his lifetime—it's essential for all close relationships, including successful marriages!

Children look to their parents to learn how to resolve conflict. During the early years, the way children relate to their peers is a reflection of their family experiences. This is especially true when it comes to dealing with conflict. Your child learns how to resolve conflicts with friends by watching how you deal with minor conflicts and daily hassles at home. Do you get emotional or remain calm? Do you direct the course of action or ask for input from others? These are important points to consider as you read the rest of this chapter.

Adults usually need to be involved when a conflict arises between young children. Careful monitoring of the conflict situation will indicate whether the children have the skills to resolve it on their own. Leaving conflict resolution in the hands of unskilled children often results in the most aggressive child's getting her way. In the long run, all the children lose. Aggressive children may learn to abuse friendships, whereas passive children may develop the "doormat" syndrome. In the section that follows we will discuss how adults can provide the guidance children need to master the art of resolving conflicts.

Parents as Conflict-Resolution Coaches

The problem for parents is finding a way to help settle conflict between young children without taking over. Although certain approaches work better than others, many challenges with peers are complicated, and there are usually several ways to solve the problem. The approach we recommend is for parents to take the role of *coach* on the sidelines and to allow children to be the key players on the field.

Children are the key players when it comes to their friendships. If children have problems with friends, parents must involve them in the process of defining the problem and picking a solution; this is how teaching works. When you are a coach and your child is a player, it's your job to support her positive efforts and to give her guidance when she begins to get into trouble. A good coach spends most of his or her time watching carefully from the sidelines as the action unfolds.

Let's look at several common mistakes that parents make in their role as coach. The first is being an *overinvolved* coach. Some parents are too quick to jump into the middle of children's problems with peers. This type of coach might say, "I don't like the way you guys are playing, and why are you talking to Sam that way? If you play with his toys, you should do what he wants . . . " Clearly, this approach doesn't help children learn to work through problems themselves.

The second extreme is being an *unaware* coach. Problems do not stir this coach to action unless the crowd roars. This type of coach might say, "Sam did what? Really? That's hard to believe; Sam's usually very easy to get along with . . . " The child in this example will have to find his own way to resolve problems with peers.

When conflicts flare up, try to view the situation as an opportunity to try out your coaching skills. An effective coach intervenes carefully, without disrupting the activity, and without criticizing or humiliating the children involved. Focus on *improving the situation* rather than trying to find out who is to blame (usually both children share responsibility). If the situation isn't too intense, you may be able to help the children resolve the conflict together; another option is to take your child aside to discuss the problem while there's still a chance to correct the situation. If tempers have flared, both children may need some time to cool down.

No Help from Mom

It's okay—my little girl can take care of herself.

Using "CPR" to Resolve Problems with Peers

This type of "CPR" is a technique you can use to help your child's friendships stay strong and healthy. There are three steps to using this type of CPR: (1) Check out everyone's point of view, (2) Plan a positive course of action, and (3) Review the plan with your child once it has been tried. You can also use this kind of CPR to revive your own social life when there's an emergency! Before using CPR, you should discuss each of these steps with your child in a supportive way. Let's take a look at how this works.

Check Out Everyone's Point of View

The first step in resolving a conflict is to check out everyone's point of view. When we get upset, we tend to become "self-focused"; we ignore the needs of others or overlook the effects of our behavior. Parents can play an important role by helping children see the bigger picture.

The scene. Dad and Mom are talking in the living room while their five-year-old son, Vicente, is playing with his best friend, Josh. Suddenly they hear Vicente yell, "Josh!" Soon after, Josh hurries out the front door and runs home.

Dad: Vicente, I need to talk to you for a minute, please.

Vicente: Okay, Dad. (He looks upset as he walks into the living room.)

Dad: What just happened in there? I heard you yelling at Josh.

Vicente: He wasn't listening to me!

Dad: (looking concerned) I wonder how he felt when you yelled?

Vicente: Pretty bad, I guess . . .

Dad: What was Josh doing when you yelled at him?

Vicente: He kept stacking the blocks, and I wanted to use them to build my fort!

Dad: Maybe we should talk about some ways you two can work it out when you don't agree.

Dad handled this friendship crisis by using the first step of CPR. His approach made it easy for Vicente to talk about what had happened, and that's a good start for understanding any conflict. Notice that Dad avoided shaming Vicente about the problem. By not shaming, blaming, or criticizing during the checkout phase, you keep your child listening and encourage cooperation. Dad also guided Vicente to the conclusion that he may have contributed to the conflict. It can be tough for parents to adopt this point of view because they naturally want to side with their child. Finally, Dad kept the discussion short; he avoided giving a lecture.

Plan a Positive Course of Action

CPR also involves *planning a course of action*. As we all know, the best way to teach is to give your child a simple, positive plan for dealing with a real-life situation. Let's see how a sensitive father might help his daughter deal with her shyness in initiating a play activity.

The scene. Dad is talking to his three-year-old daughter, Charmaine, who is trying to get to know the other kids in the apartment complex they just moved into. They're outside washing the car.

Dad: What's the matter, girl? You look kind of sad.

Charmaine: No one wants to play with me.

Dad: What? I can't believe that! Hey, there's Lauren. Have you tried playing with her?

Charmaine: (She just shakes her head.)

Dad: Do you know what to do?

Charmaine: (She shakes her head again.)

Dad: Here's an idea: Why don't you go over there (pointing to the playground) and see if she wants to play with your new ball.

Charmaine: (no response)

Dad: (smiling) Here, let's practice. I'll be Lauren, and you ask me to play.

Charmaine: (holds up the ball) Do you want to play?

Dad: Sure. Here, throw it to me!

Charmaine: (laughs)

Dad: Let's walk down there so you can ask her, okay? (Charmaine looks up and takes his hand, and they walk toward the playground.)

In this scene, Dad gave Charmaine just enough support to help her overcome her shyness and ask Lauren to play. One of the most useful things he did was to *role-play* the situation with her—he played her role to show her what to do. This gave Charmaine the confidence she needed to take the next step and actually initiate play. Teaching social skills is the same as teaching a young child any new skill, such as setting the table. The best approach is to walk them through it. Older preschool children will not remember more than two steps even under the best of circumstances, but they can learn a skill if you keep the steps simple and help them practice it several times. As a general rule, the younger the child, the smaller each of the CPR steps should be.

Now let's go back to the earlier scene involving Vicente and Josh and their conflict over the blocks. Mom has decided to teach Vicente *negotiation* skills that he can use to prevent a similar situation from arising in the future. She wisely picks a time when Vicente is not upset.

The scene. Mom and Vicente are in the kitchen talking about the problem he had when he was playing with Josh.

Mom: Vicente, let's talk about what happened with Josh for a little bit.

Vicente: (looking a little reluctant) O-o-kay.

Mom: Let's say I'm Josh and I'm playing with the blocks. Now you decide that you want to play superheroes. What do you say? (Mom pretends to stack blocks.)

Vicente: Josh! I wanted to use those for my spaceship!

Mom: (trying to stay neutral and sincere) Vicente, do you think I'm going to want to play your game if you talk to me that way?

Vicente: I guess not.

Mom: It would be better to say something like "Hey, Josh, let's use the blocks for spaceships!" (said enthusiastically with a smile) Now you try.

Vicente: Okay. "Josh, do you want to use the blocks for superhero spaceships?"

Mom: (smiling) That's great!

Vicente: But what if he says no?

Mom: Well, let's see what might happen. You be Josh and say no.

Vicente: "No."

Mom: "Okay, what do you want to do?"

Vicente: "Build a bridge."

Mom: "How about building a superhero space station that we can play with instead. Here, you can have this guy, and I'll take the other one."

Vicente: Okay!

Mom: Great. I think that approach will work much better. If you guys can *cooperate,* you can have a lot more fun together.

Think about trying to explain to Vicente *why* these skills would work. Would he understand? It was especially important that Mom gave a label—cooperation—for the skill she was trying to teach. In the future, Vicente will have a better understanding of what this term means.

Not surprisingly, the way you use CPR with a two-year-old is different from the way you use it with four- and five-year-olds. With very young children, it's best to keep it simple. At this age, you need to identify the problem behavior, model the positive behavior you want to see in its place, and teach the word that describes the positive behavior. This approach is illustrated in the following example.

The scene. Todd and Britt are playing together on the living room floor; both children are two years old. Mom sees Britt hit Todd on the head and grab his toy car, and she decides to take advantage of this opportunity to teach a new skill.

Mom: (firmly and without anger) Britt, no hitting. (She kneels down and takes the toy away from him.) Now I want you to ask Todd nicely (she hands the toy car back to Todd), "Can I have the car, please?"

Britt: Caw please?

Todd: No.

Mom: Okay, Britt. You play with the truck instead, and in a few minutes you can play with the car.

Todd: (hands the car to Britt)

Mom: That was nice, Todd. Now Britt, say thank you to Todd.

Britt: Tank yew.

Mom: Good job! Now give Todd the truck so he has something to play with.

Britt: (gives the truck to Todd)

Mom: Good job! (with a big smile and enthusiasm) You two are *sharing!*

If at first you don't succeed, don't lose sight of your goal. Although Mom did a good job of responding to the situation, it often takes young children some time to make the transition to the positive behavior you are requesting. When Mom made it clear that the car would have to be shared in a few minutes, Todd decided to offer it to Britt. This set the stage for Britt's sharing, and Mom gave them both positive attention for doing a good job. Everyone wins, and these young children have taken another step in developing an important social skill.

Review the Plan with Your Child

The last step of the CPR approach is to review the plan with your child. This is very important. To review the plan, you need to watch children play to see how they are doing. When you see them in action, you need to remember your role as coach and try not to be either overly involved or too detached. There are two actions you can take. One is to *support* your child for displaying any part of the skill you were teaching. The other is to *repeat the CPR process* at the right time. Don't be surprised if you need to repeat CPR many times before your child uses the complete skill. If your child doesn't seem to be improving, maybe you are expecting too much, or perhaps the situation is bad and you need to structure a healthier play environment.

Teaching children to negotiate with other children may be a long-term project. For example, helping siblings get along is usually a recurring theme. In most situations, however, you should be able to see some progress and offer support. Let's see how this works in the following example.

The scene. It's one week later and Vicente is playing with another friend, Jake. Mom and Dad overhear Vicente politely asking his friend what he wants to do. The two children negotiate an activity that they both enjoy, and they begin playing together in the next room. Dad doesn't want to interrupt them, so he waits until Vicente runs through the living room to check in with him (Jake is playing in the next room).

Dad: (speaking softly) Hey, bud, come here a second. (Vicente turns and comes over to his father.) I heard you guys playing in there. You're doing a great job of cooperating!

Vicente: (obviously pleased with himself) Thanks, Dad!

Dad: Hey, I was going to take the truck to the dump (one of Vicente's favorite activities). Do you want to ask Jake if he wants to come along?

Vicente: Yeah, I'll go see!

Parental support is always important for maintaining new skills. The dad in this scene did an outstanding job of providing support by using good timing, giving verbal praise, and adding a bonus reward of doing something special with the boys. Because of Dad's efforts, Vicente is more likely to use negotiation skills with his friends in the future.

Fine-Tuning CPR

How should you intervene in the review stage when things don't go well? The first rule is to be constructive, to avoid shaming or criticizing. Be careful; even lighthearted humor that has a hint of teasing can hurt the feelings of young children and discourage them from using you as a resource later. The best approach is to repeat the checkout and planning stages with your child when it's a good time.

In an earlier example, three-year-old Charmaine wanted to make a new friend at the apartment complex. Let's rejoin them.

The scene. Before Charmaine could ask Lauren to play on the playground, a third child joined Lauren and started to play with her. Dad watched as the two children ignored Charmaine standing there with her new ball. This was a painful experience for both Dad and Charmaine. Dad walks up to Charmaine as she turns and walks away from the playground.

Charmaine: (with tears running down her cheeks) She didn't want to play . . .

Dad: I guess that other little girl got there first. That's too bad. I'll bet that makes you sad.

Charmaine: (Now crying loudly, she nods her head in agreement.)

Dad: Hey, why don't you sit on my shoulders and we'll take a walk. (Charmaine climbs onto his shoulders.) You know, I think I know what happened.

Charmaine: (a little calmer now) What?

Dad: Lauren's friend had just asked her to play, and they were starting a new game. Did you see that?

Charmaine: Yeah.

Dad: (more lighthearted) I don't think they saw you standing over there, girl! (Charmaine doesn't respond.) I think they were so busy with their game that they didn't know you were talking to them. You want to know something?

Charmaine: What?

Dad: I think you gave it a good try. I'm proud of you. (Charmaine doesn't respond.)

Depending on Charmaine's mood and how she rebounds, this may be enough discussion for now. The important thing for Dad is to help Charmaine have a broader view of the event so she is less likely to see it as a rejection. If Charmaine rebounds quickly from this accidental rebuff, Dad could help her plan a different strategy for initiating play with two or more children. These strategies include asking politely if she can join in or asking about the game they are playing. For a sensitive child, however, it may be better for her to practice initiating play with one child because entering a group is riskier.

Summary

Young children need help from their parents as they learn to build and maintain friendships with their peers. By assuming the role of coach, parents can be involved in this delicate process without taking over. Children need support as they develop three kinds of social skills: (1) initiating play, (2) sharing and cooperation, and (3) conflict resolution. As you watch the action from the sidelines, you'll see that sometimes children can take care of their own problems. But when your child could use some help, it's time to use the CPR approach outlined in this chapter. The C stands for checking out others' points of view, the P for planning a solution, and the R for reviewing with your child how the plan is working.

When parents use this approach, they need to be supportive of their children, while at the same time helping them grow beyond their current strengths and weaknesses. As children grow older, they must gradually learn to take charge of their own social lives. The efforts you put into coaching your children's friendships at an early age will set the stage for success as your children enter the complex world of peers.

• • • • • • • • • • •

Home Practice Activity

Basic Skill (Time required: 20 minutes)
We strongly recommend that you and another adult practice role-playing a typical conflict scene before attempting to coach your child. Let's say that your four-year-old daughter is playing with a friend, and they start to argue about what to do next. One child wants to play "mommy and baby," and the other wants to ride Hot Wheels in the driveway. Play the part of the parent while the other adult pretends to be the child; make the role-playing exercise as realistic as possible. Use CPR to resolve this situation (check out the other person's point of view, make a plan to resolve the problem, and review the plan to see how it is working). Practice using CPR the wrong way first—try to make the "child" feel blamed and humiliated. What were some of the things you did or said that made the other person feel blamed or criticized? Then practice using CPR the right way. Ask the other adult for feedback on the things you did or said that made him or her feel that you were being constructive and supportive.

Advanced Skill (Time required: 45 minutes)
It takes practice to be a good coach. The first step is to develop a CPR plan by filling out the Coaching Skills Worksheet that follows. Think of a recent conflict your child experienced that would have been a good choice for CPR. You know your child best—is he more likely to have problems with initiating, sharing and cooperation, or conflict resolution? Pick the issue that seems to occur most often. Describe the situation in words that are comfortable for you. This exercise will help you think through how you would approach each step with your child. If you're ready to give it a try, simply follow the directions on the worksheet!

Coaching Skills Worksheet

Completed by _____ Date _____

Describe a recent conflict with peers involving your child. (Who was involved, what was the issue, and what was the situation?) _____

_____

_____

_____

What questions could you ask to help your child check out the other child's point of view? (For example, "How do you think Amanda felt when you refused to share your toy?") _____

_____

_____

Describe a plan that you think would resolve the situation. (For example, taking turns) _____

_____

_____

How could you guide your child to come to the same conclusion? Use statements and questions. (For example, "How do you think taking turns would work?") _____

_____

_____

How would you know whether the plan is working? (For example, watch your child in play situations and track successes/difficulties with sharing and cooperation; comment on your child's successes, and use CPR to resolve conflicts.) _____

_____

_____

CHAPTER EIGHT

Building Family Relationships

The scene. It's a beautiful day, and Mom and Dad are out for a walk with their four-year-old son, Kobin, and their big yellow dog. As they walk past a field of tall grass, Dad finds some sticks for Kobin to throw for the dog. Mom and Dad talk and laugh as they watch the dog fetching sticks for Kobin. The pace is relaxed and comfortable, and the family is enjoying spending time together.

This scene captures the joy of being a family. Experiences like this help family members appreciate one another and grow closer. There are some added benefits as well; having fun together is like getting a booster shot that keeps the family healthy when problems come up. Shared activities build strong family relationships at several levels: They improve how you relate to your children and your partner, and they contribute to your happiness and sense of well-being as an individual. In the following section we'll take a closer look at how this works.

The "Feeling Good" Savings Account

A family is a fragile thing; it takes care and nurturing to keep it strong. A useful way to think about this is to imagine that your family has a "feeling good" savings account. When you do things together that everyone enjoys, you are making a deposit in the family's feeling good savings account. Deposits to the account come in all shapes and sizes—including special events such as trips to Disneyland and simple things such as talking about the events of the day at dinnertime.

When children are a little older, shared activities make big deposits in the family's account. Playing baseball in the park, watching your child's school play, going camping, and doing other activities together builds a strong foundation for long-term family relationships. (This can make a big difference during the teenage years!) It also helps your children develop skills that they will continue to use as adults and that, it is hoped, they will teach their children. This is one of the ways that basic values are passed along from one generation to the next.

Setting the Stage for Shared Activities

The feeling good savings account becomes particularly important when things aren't going so well. When your family is faced with daily hassles, conflict, and crises, you are making withdrawals from the account.[1] If you make too many withdrawals and not enough deposits, the tension level increases and family members become irritable and stop caring for one another. It's that simple.

The balance in your feeling good savings account shows the overall well-being of your family. The best way to maintain a healthy balance is to make regular deposits through shared activities. The earlier your family starts having fun together, the better.

Building the Couple's Account

Your relationship as a couple is the wellspring of support for the entire family, and it too needs to be nurtured. Unfortunately, couples with small children tend to focus all of their attention on the children and neglect the relationship that holds the two of them *and the family* together. Unless you put some effort into your relationship, the good feelings you have about your partner will begin to fade. If you don't seem to be getting along with your partner, your sex life is dismal, and you get into arguments or have simply stopped talking, it means that your account is overdrawn!

New parents often become isolated from their friends because they are busy caring for the baby. Guilt plays a major role here. How could you leave your infant with a baby-sitter just because you want to go out and have fun? What kind of parent would do that? Focusing on the baby and ignoring your own needs seems like the noble thing to do. Couples often stop doing the activities they used to enjoy together for months or even years after their first baby is born. Gradually they begin to feel like tired roommates who are trapped in their roles as parents. You can take steps to avoid this situation by talking with your partner about making your relationship a higher priority. Then you can develop a plan to share

---

[1]*Tom's note:* a little humor can also help to diffuse a tense situation. When things weren't going well for us, we would sing a song that went something like this: "We've got problems—gnarly problems—who could ask for anything more?" and we would all laugh.

quality time together on a regular basis; for example, every Friday night could be Mom and Dad's night out.

Here's another way to put the love back in your relationship. This approach was developed by marriage therapists to help distressed couples regain their good feelings toward one another. What were some of the things that you and your partner used to do for each other that made you fall in love in the first place? It certainly wasn't changing diapers and mowing the lawn! Your list might include things such as giving flowers, buying a special book or CD that your partner would enjoy, giving each other a massage, going sailing, or spending the day together at the beach. Now we're going to ask you to make one day every month a "love day." The way this works is that you make a commitment to do five things that will make your partner feel good and show that you think he or she is special. If each partner does this every other month, you'll be surprised at the difference a few thoughtful gestures and sharing some time together as a couple can make. It will rekindle your marriage and help you be better partners *and* better parents!

Building Individual Accounts

A family is made up of individuals who also deserve to have some personal time. In this close-knit system, it's easy to see how the attitude, energy, and behavior of each person has an impact on the entire family. When you do things that you personally enjoy, such as going for a walk or visiting a friend, it adds to the balance in your individual account. By setting aside some personal time, you will be developing coping resources that extend beyond the immediate family, providing a broader support system to draw on when you face personal challenges at work or at home.

Single-parent families are even more at risk because they have fewer resources to help them cope with the demands of child rearing and running a household. Without a partner to help them, single parents have to rely on good friends and immediate family to fill the gap.

You need to be reasonably happy to build positive relationships with your partner, children, and friends. The superman/superwoman concept belongs in comic books. No one can ignore his or her own needs forever. If the only thing you do is work and take care of everyone else, stress will catch up with you sooner or later. Over time, you will lose your sense of humor and become irritable, resentful, unhappy, or depressed. Studies have shown that depression is a serious problem for mothers of young children; the depression usually begins when the first child is born, and it continues until the children enter grade school. When family members go through difficult times and don't handle it well, they make withdrawals from the family's sense of well-being. This suggests that doing the things you enjoy isn't entirely selfish.

As with most things in life, the ultimate challenge is to keep everything in balance by caring for your children, nurturing your relationship with your spouse, and taking some personal time for yourself. Although it may take some planning to make deposits in all of your accounts, it's well worth it. Nothing is more important than creating a healthy family atmosphere for your children!

Now that we have taken a look at how shared activities affect the adult relationships in your family, let's turn our attention to strategies for building relationships with your children.

Making the Most of Shared Activities

The scene. Mom is in the living room with her three-year-old son, Cyrus. She's reading the newspaper while Cyrus is playing with blocks on the floor.

Cyrus: (He's busy making motorboat sounds as he pushes a block across the floor. He stops when he gets to the coffee table and looks up at his mom.) Mommy, will you play with me now?

Mom: (briefly looking up from her newspaper) Just a minute, honey, I'm reading.

Cyrus: (looking upset) Come on, Mom, I need someone to play with!

Mom: Oh, okay. (Reluctantly she puts her newspaper on the couch and sits on the floor near Cyrus.) What do you want to do?

Cyrus: (pushing the block across the floor) It's a motorboat, just like Uncle John's!

Mom: (As she looks on, it's clear that she doesn't know what to do next.)

The mother in this scene wants to spend some quality time playing with her little boy. Playing together would be fun for both of them. Oddly enough, as adults, we are sometimes challenged by simply playing! Your relationship with your child depends on the success of shared activities, whether it's playing, doing a project, or just spending time together. Even routine chores such as going shopping or working in the yard can turn into interesting and fun learning experiences. Being a parent of a young child teaches us to look at these activities with a fresh perspective. Does playing take skill? You bet it does!

In this chapter we focus on three types of quality-time activities you can share with toddlers and preschoolers: (1) child-directed play, (2) story time, and (3) shared routine activities. Let's begin by taking a closer look at adult-child play.

Child-Directed Play

It's often difficult for us to appreciate what it feels like to be a child. If we could see the world from a child's point of view, we would immediately notice that parents are in control of everything. Children also have a need to practice and enjoy having some control in their lives. Play time is one of the few situations in which the child can be in charge of the activity.

Adults mistakenly tend to think that children are wasting time when they are playing. This is unfortunate because play gives children a chance to try out new ideas, develop coordination and social skills, and learn about the world around them. Children need to play with other children and with adults as well. Research has shown that adult-child play is important because it provides special opportunities for children to develop language, problem-solving, self-esteem, and relationship skills.

What is the parents' role in child-directed play? As we will see, it's a new role for parents because the child gets to make most of the decisions. We recommend that you try this approach because it offers several advantages for the child. First, it allows the child to explore her imagination and be creative without adult-imposed limitations. Second, it gives the child an opportunity to express her view of the world. You may be surprised at the way she sees her friends, family, and other important events in her life. Third, it gives you a chance to relax and go with the flow—to let go of the burdens associated with being an adult. We are not suggesting that you should become a child again—you have much to offer as a mature adult.

The Parents' Role in Child-Directed Play

In the following section we will discuss five tips for participating in child-directed play: (1) Follow the child's lead, (2) Encourage imagination, (3) Describe what the child is doing, (4) Don't be afraid to act silly, and (5) Take small steps. These tips will help you to join in play activities with your child without taking over or watching passively from the sidelines. Let's consider each of them in more detail.

1. Follow the child's lead. Adults easily become impatient because the pace of child-directed play is too slow, or because the child wants to repeat part of the activity over and over again. Keep in mind that *this is an opportunity for the child to take charge, and your role is to simply join in and be involved.* Let the child dictate the pace and type of activity. You can gently guide the process by asking questions and adding details. For example, if your little girl wants to pretend she's driving a car, you could grab a round pillow and say, "Let's use this as the steering wheel!" Then show how you would hold the pillow like a steering wheel and hand it to her; after that, you could add a horn (perhaps a tennis ball would work for this), and so on. In this way the child feels in control of the activity, and you are an active participant. Although you may be tempted, *don't take over the activity.*

2. Encourage imagination. Children love to exercise their imaginations, and with a little help, almost anything is possible. Children usually begin to show signs of make-believe play by the time they are two or three years old.

Some adults seem to think that fantasy play is bad for the mental health of their children, but studies have shown just the opposite—make-believe play gives children a safe place to try out new ideas and work things out for themselves. If your two-year-old wants to pretend that the couch is a train, go with it. Make train noises, imagine that you are going over a bridge and what that would be like, pretend there's a cow (or an elephant!) on the tracks up ahead, and so on.

Art activities also help children develop their creativity. Make sure that you have lots of crayons, paper, and other materials readily available. Don't worry too much about *teaching* art, simply spend time doing it.

3. Describe what the child is doing. Another great way for parents to stay involved in a child's play activity is to provide a running commentary on the action. It sounds something like a sports announcer. You might say, "And now Miss Piggy is getting dressed for a party. Nice hat! Where is she going tonight?" This shows the child that you are interested in what she is doing, and it prompts the child to join in and fill in some of the details. This is a much better approach than simply asking a string of questions (for example, "What is Miss Piggy doing now? Is that her favorite hat? Where is she going?"), which is what many adults do in this situation. Although asking questions also shows that you're interested, it can be overwhelming for the child. Try to focus on describing the activity, pace your comments so your child has plenty of chances to join in, and perhaps ask a question every now and then.

You may not think this tip is important, but toddlers and preschoolers learn to use language in these situations. For example, when you say, "Hey, look, Miss Piggy lost her hat!" you have just taught both the content of language and how it's used to express ideas. As adults, we often forget that these shared activities provide important opportunities for children to learn the basics of communication!

4. Don't be afraid to act silly. Playing with young children may involve making motorboat sounds or dressing up like a superhero with a "cape" made of a towel stuffed into the back of your shirt. Some adults feel foolish doing this, even though they realize it's just for fun. It's healthy for you to act silly every once in a while—it will help you avoid the adult malady of taking things too seriously. Who cares if the neighbors see you running around the house having fun? They probably wish they could cut loose and act silly every now and then. Having kids is also a good excuse to buy the toys you always wanted as a child. Now you can walk into the store and buy five rockets and tell the store clerk it's for your little girl. The clerk will just smile.

5. Take small steps. If you are one of those adults who find it challenging to follow these steps in child-directed play, don't be too hard on yourself. With practice, your skill and comfort level will improve. You may want to take small steps as you try these skills, until you and your child are more comfortable with this approach to playing. For example, five minutes of child-directed play is a healthy start. Try to improve the *quality* of your adult-child play before worrying about how much time you devote to it.

Now let's take a look at some other shared activities that build parent-child relationships and add to the feeling good savings account. Specifically, we'll discuss story time and shared routine activities, which are typically not child-directed activities. With some ingenuity, however, children can play an active role in these important family events as well.

Story Time

Most parents know that it's important to spend time reading books with their children. Research indicates that reading to young children helps them to develop language and critical thinking skills. In fact, simply counting the number of children's books in a family's home will give you a fairly accurate picture of a child's readiness for school.

The first step is to pick a story that is appropriate to your child's age and interests. Keep in mind that the purpose of story time is to have fun. Let the child choose the story and the pace of the reading. Allow plenty of time for exploring ideas—don't forget to exercise your imagination too! Children often will enjoy reading the same story over and over again. To them, it's like entering a whole new world. For more variety, go to the library or a bookstore and pick up some new books every now and then. Children ages three and up will enjoy going with you, and looking for new books can become a shared activity that you both look forward to.

Make story time part of the family routine. Pick a time each day to sit down together and read at least one short book or part of a story. Especially good times are before naps and bedtime. Reading is an incentive for children to get ready for bed. It's a calming activity that helps children rest, and it's a wonderful way to get close at the end of a long, sometimes stressful day.

A good children's story often offers a message about relationships and basic values, such as the merits of telling the truth. Of course, you can build on these teaching opportunities by asking questions as you read the story. You might ask, "How did Sister Bear feel when Brother Bear said that?" "Is Sister Bear getting bossy now?" "Is that a good way to make friends?" and so on. These questions will help your child understand the friendship skills discussed in Chapter Seven. Another way to build on the story is to close the book for a few moments while you and your child try to guess what's going to happen next.

During story time, you and your child can look at the world together. If story time is fun and you're having good discussions, then it's working. If either of you is losing interest, pick a new book, use more emotion when reading, or stop and ask a question. If you listen carefully, your child will tell you what needs to happen to make story time work better.

On occasion, you may want to try switching roles during story time, especially with books you both have come to know by heart.[2] Role switching gives your child a chance to practice all of the subtle reading skills you have long taken for granted: sequencing a story, using emotion to communicate ideas, and relating pictures to words. Also, if you watch carefully, your child may reveal some interesting details about his or her view of you as a parent.

Shared Routine Activities

In many parts of the world, children actively participate in their parents' lives, both at home and at work. We think it's important for today's parents to involve their children in their daily lives, even in the toddler and preschool years. We should be concerned about letting other adults raise

---

[2]*Scot's note:* This was a favorite game when I read bedtime stories with my youngest son, Kobin. Although he was only four years old, Kobin enjoyed playing the dad while I played the role of the child. Kobin couldn't actually read the book, but he knew the story well enough to make it up as he turned the pages. The best part of all was that I would ask the same questions that Kobin often asked during story time: "But, D-a-a-d, *why* did the troll live under the bridge?" Then we would both laugh and go on with the story.

our children in daycare centers and preschools because no one can match the commitment of a concerned parent when it comes to caring for a child's welfare. Unfortunately, in many families, both parents have jobs outside the home, and opportunities for spending time with children are limited. Our modern lifestyle has taken its toll on the well-being of our children. Although there is no simple solution to this problem, we suggest that sharing routine activities is a good way to bring the worlds of parents and children closer together.

Restructuring adult tasks so that children can be involved is called *scaffolding*. A scaffold lifts a person up to make difficult tasks easier. As parents, adults have to provide scaffolding to make it possible for young children to be involved in daily routine activities. The basic idea is to slow down the pace of the task and try to make it more engaging for the child. In general, the younger the child, the slower the pace. Let's see how scaffolding works in the following example.

The scene. It's Friday afternoon, and Mom has taken her three-year-old son, Jered, out of daycare so they can spend some quiet time at home. Tired from her long week at work, Mom was looking forward to having the afternoon to relax, but the afternoon has slipped away, and now it's time to go to the grocery store. Mom decides to make the most of the shopping trip by involving Jered in the activity.

Mom: Okay, big fella, let's go to the store. Let's see—I wonder what we need at the store. I'd better make a list. Jered, can you find some paper up on the shelf?

Jered: (Excited to help, he runs over to get a piece of paper and brings it back.)

Mom: (sitting at the kitchen table) Thank you! Let's see. We need toilet paper, milk, and something for dinner. (looking at Jered) Can you think of anything else?

Jered: (with enthusiasm) Juice!

Mom: Oh, that's right. Thanks for reminding me! Okay . . . (adding it to her list) Oops, we can't forget Moonlight (the cat). She needs something for dinner, too! Anything else? (Mom notices that Jered is losing interest.) Okay, I think that's it. Will you please draw a picture on the shopping list for me while I get ready?

Jered: Okay. (He takes Mom's pen and sets to work.)

Mom: (It's 15 minutes later, and Mom and Jered are at the store. As she puts Jered in the shopping cart, she hands him the list.) Ready, set, let's go! Now I need your help. When we find the things we're looking for, you check them off the list. Okay?

This mom is doing a good job of scaffolding. Even though she wasn't looking forward to shopping, she made it fun for both of them by taking the extra time to keep her child involved. In effect, this extended their quality time together. Sharing activities with children also teaches them daily living skills that we tend to take for granted as adults. As an added benefit, children are less likely to misbehave if you find ways to engage their interest in your daily routines.

Scaffolding is a delicate process. Notice that to make it work, the mother in this example had to control her own mood. If she had been irritable about going to the store, it would have been very difficult to engage Jered in the activity. She also had to think of some things that Jered could do to help, such as crossing items off the list while they were shopping. It's important to use a game-like approach that is as upbeat and positive as possible. Having Jered draw a picture on the shopping list was a good way to keep him absorbed and cooperative, even though the picture wasn't necessary from a practical standpoint.

Realistically, only some of your activities can be approached in this way. The key is not to be in a hurry—*even though involving children in adult activities slows things down, it's well worth your time.* Including children in daily tasks at an early age sets the stage for you and your children to enjoy doing things together for many years to come. The list of activities that can be set up as shared tasks is almost endless: doing dishes (pull up a stool), going to work with a parent for part of the day, exercising, sweeping the patio, going to the lumberyard, and washing the car. Just use a little ingenuity.

Summary

Family relationships are at the heart of family life. They determine how you feel about one another and how you feel about yourself as well. Simply stated, positive and healthy relationships depend on shared activities. We introduced the idea of the feeling good family savings account to help you understand how to create a family lifestyle that promotes the well-being of all family members. Whether you are trying to make a good situation better or deal with recurring problems, making deposits in your family's account by spending quality time together is a good place to start.

We also discussed the importance of play and the parents' role in child-directed play. Five tips were offered for playing with children: (1) Follow the child's lead, (2) Encourage imagination, (3) Describe what the child is doing, (4) Don't be afraid to act silly, and (5) Take small steps. These tips will help you enrich the quality of the time you spend playing with your child.

Two other quality-time activities were discussed: story time and shared routine activities. The related concept of scaffolding was introduced to show you how to involve your children in daily tasks by restructuring and slowing down the pace of the activity. Now it's your turn to relax and have some fun!

• • • • • • • • • • •

Home Practice Activity

Basic Skill (Time required: 10 minutes)
Pick a time to practice child-directed play. Make sure you're not in a hurry. For the next 5 or 10 minutes, let your child make the decisions about the *type* of play and *your role* in the activity. Use the tips for playing with children discussed in this chapter (listed below). After you have finished, circle the tips that you used during the activity. How did it feel? Did your child seem to enjoy the activity?

Tips for playing with children:

1. Follow the child's lead.

2. Encourage imagination.

3. Describe what the child is doing.

4. Don't be afraid to act silly.

5. Take small steps.

Advanced Skill (Time required: all you can give!)
If you're not doing this already, pick a time of day for you and your child to read together. Also, check to make sure your partner has also set aside some reading time. This is a great activity that the whole family can enjoy together!

Now try to think of two routine activities that you could restructure so that your toddler or preschooler could become more involved. What types of tasks can you let your child do? Use the lines provided to write down your ideas. Then give it a try! What did your child enjoy most about the activity? What did you enjoy most?

Describe a routine activity and how it could be restructured to involve your child:

1. _____
_____
_____

2. _____
_____
_____

Closing Remarks

As this book draws to a close, we want to acknowledge the investment you have made in your family's future. Having a family is a big responsibility, and the fact that you are willing to read books and try new ideas is to your credit. It is our hope that some of the advice we have given here will help you create the kind of family life that you imagined when you first learned that a child was on the way. Those dreams are important and should become part of your family's heritage. We invite you to write to us at the address given on the title page so that we can take your successes and challenges into consideration when we revise this book. Best wishes for a bright future!

About the Authors

Thomas J. Dishion received his Ph.D. in clinical psychology from the University of Oregon. His interests include understanding the development of antisocial behavior and substance abuse in children and adolescents, as well as designing effective interventions and prevention programs. In particular, he has conducted research on the contribution of peer and parenting dynamics to child and adolescent social and emotional development. His intervention research focuses on the effectiveness of family-centered interventions. He is the founder and director of research at the Child and Family Center and professor of clinical psychology, both at the University of Oregon. Prior to that, he was a research scientist at the Oregon Social Learning Center. He has published over 90 scientific reports and three books for professionals working and conducting research with troubled children and their families. For recreation, Tom enjoys a daily run on the trails of Eugene, time with his family, and the Oregon outdoors.

Scot G. Patterson is a writer and editor with a B.S. in psychology. During the past 25 years, he has collaborated on a variety of academic and scholarly publications dealing with parenting issues, delinquency, and the treatment of depression. With Dr. Gerald R. Patterson and Dr. Marion Forgatch, Scot was instrumental in creating the best-selling books *Parents and Adolescents Living Together* (Parts 1 and 2), available

115

from Research Press. His other writing projects include children's books and science fiction for middle school readers. Scot lives and works in Eugene, Oregon, where he enjoys tennis, ballroom dancing, skiing, and impressionist oil painting. He has two children, Miles and Kobin.